STAR GRAPHIC DESIGNERS

Books are to be returned on
th...

STAR GRAPHIC DESIGNERS

Cristina Paredes

LOFT

Star Graphic Designers

Editorial coordinator: Cristian Campos
Editor and Texts: Cristina Paredes
English translation: Cillero & de Motta
Art director: Emma Termes
Layout & cover design: Maira Purman

© 2012 LOFT Publications
Via Laietana 32, 4th fl., of. 104
08003 Barcelona, Spain
Tel.: +34 93 268 80 88
Fax: +34 93 268 70 73
loft@loftpublications.com
www.loftpublications.com

ISBN: 978-84-9936-883-2

Printed in China

I'M A STAR

THE HENLEY COLLEGE LIBRARY

"Graphic design has become
the fabric of contemporary
image and figure of the
multidisciplinary designer has
become the leading figure
that captures the reality."

Graphic design is an evolving discipline. Since William Addison Dwiggins in 1922 used the term graphic design to describe the organization of the elements to be reproduced on paper (typography, white space, ornaments and images), many things have changed and the traditional approach has given way to IT tools that multiply the creative possibilities by a thousand. However, the advent of technology does not prevent the usual inaccurate considerations about this practice. It has gone from considering that graphic design is an applied art to believing that anyone with a command of programs such as InDesign or Photoshop can be considered a designer.

This could not be further from the truth. Graphic design is a discipline that offers solutions to specific communication needs, which involves solving problems, expressing ideas and, ultimately, creating a great intellectual exercise.

The current experimental limits of graphic design means it is more accurate to speak of visual communication. Now designers foray into other disciplines such as music, art, photography, illustration or editing, which dilutes the boundaries of design. In addition, the daring nature of many artists allows them to explore different aesthetics and different ways of conveying a message, deviating from the commercial effectiveness of the work. And although their work is considered transgressive or is initially rejected, it is incorporated into modern imagery.

Graphic design has become the fabric of contemporary image and figure of the multidisciplinary designer has become the leading figure that captures the reality and improves the focus of a design to make it work and to better communicate the message. What challenge do graphic designers face today? One of the keys is to be original in a global environment, achieve and maintain an identity when many references, either musical or from the movies, are common in most countries. Another continues to be finding the balance between what the client demands and creativity, between the formality of an order and the freedom to push the boundaries.

This collection of work shows that, despite global campaigns for major brands, the local cultural and social references have not been lost along the way. The designers selected for this book, which could have been many more, are authors bursting with creativity. Their proposals show different visual languages aimed at communicating and surprising.

2xGoldstein

Rheinstetten, Germany
www.2xgoldstein.de

We, 2xGoldstein, are twins, parents, and also graphic designers. We studied at the University of Art and Design in Karlsruhe (HfG) with the lecturers Gunter Rambow and Melk Imboden. At present we are dedicated primarily to the design of books, posters and logos for different publishers, museums and other cultural institutions. In addition to all this activity, we teach poster design at the University of Applied Sciences Bielefeld.

Poster for the 5th edition of Adam Seide Day of Literature, in which three writers are invited to readings and discussions.

Poster for the annual meeting of INMM (Institute for Music and Music Education).

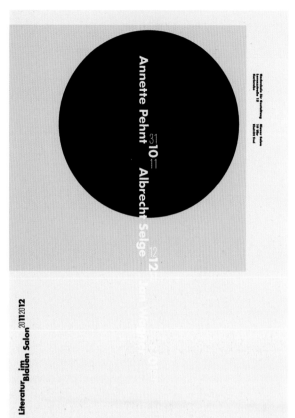

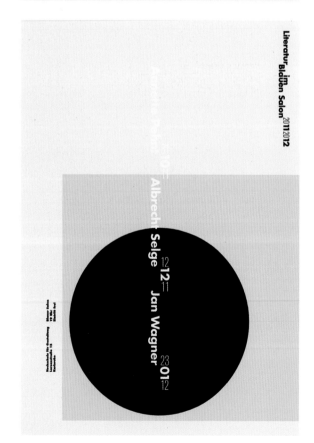

Literatur
im
Blauen Salon

26/4
Anne
Weber

10/5
Günter
Hack

14/6
Monika
Rinck

Jeweils
montags
19 Uhr

HfG
Karlsruhe

Poster design for conferences *Literature in the Blue Room*, in which every three months three writers are presented at the University of Art and Design in Karlsruhe. The birds are Buchfinken, which are "chaffinches" in German. Serigraph on fabric.

Poster for a series of lectures on American cinema and architecture at the University of Kaiserslautern.

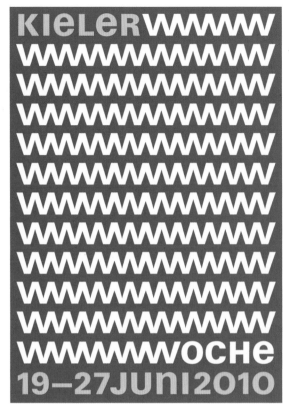

1

2

1. Poster for Kieler Woche 2010. Kieler Woche is one of the largest sailing regattas in the world, as well as a summer festival.

2. Design for the exposition *Mut zur Wut*, by the German designer Götz Gramlich. The poster is entitled *Constructuve Converter*.

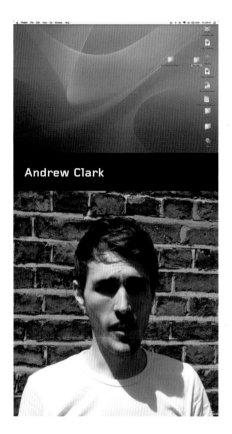

Andrew Clark

London, UK
www.thisisandrewclark.com

I am an illustrator and graphic designer from the countryside village of Clayton in West Yorkshire. I operate out of London having originally moved to the capital to study Illustration at Camberwell College of Arts. Having graduated, I built an early fan-base within the London design community through a series of internships, competition wins and sponsored exhibitions with fashion labels and advertising agencies. The majority of my regular work comes from a range of magazines from the UK, USA and Europe. I'm also pleased to have worked with clients in Asia and hope to continue building working-relationships globally.

Illustrations for the magazine *Wallpaper* about sustainability issues and the Milan Furniture Fair.

Conceptual drawings carried out for animation projects.

Personal and experimental projects inspired by childhood trips or games.

Illustration for the cover of USA magazine *AR* with the portrait of billionaire John Arnold.

1. Illustrations designed for the book entitled *The Clark Alphabet*, a conceptual book about the notion of the alphabet. Each letter is a drawing and once deciphered, texts can be read, just like a secret code.

2. Illustration about cycling on the streets of Rawalpindi created for the magazine *The Ride*.

3. Commemorative poster for the creative agency Dixon Baxi, who invited 25 designers and illustrators to collaborate on the project *Join the Dots*, which reinterprets the symbol of the full stop.

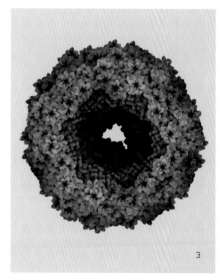

Andy Smith

Hastings, UK
www.asmithillustration.com

I am an illustrator based in Hastings in the UK. Educated at the Royal College of Art, London my clients include Nike, Orange, Sony PSP, Mercedes and McDonalds. My work often involves a combination of illustration and typography and has a humorous, optimistic and energetic feel. I have a background in screen printing which informs what I do and lends my imagery a hand made, hand printed, tactile feel. As well as producing commercial work for clients I also enjoy screen printing posters and books which I have exhibited in the UK, USA, France and Australia.

One of the limited edition serigraphs for the individual exhibition *Sunny Side Up*.

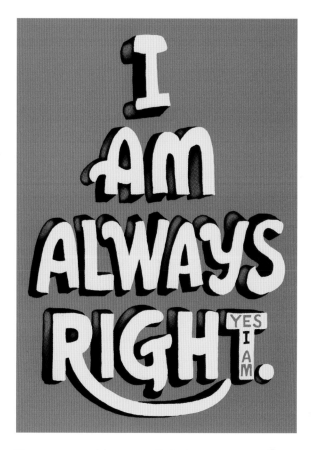

These screen prints were exhibited at the Soma Gallery in Bristol, UK.

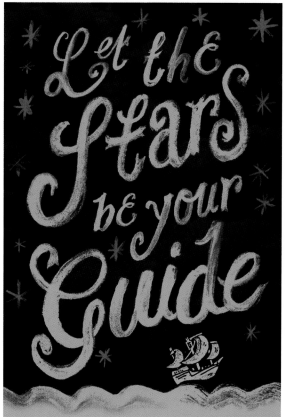

CAPTAIN ROBERT FALCON SCOTT ARRIVES AT THE SOUTH POLE, 17 JANUARY 1912.

Andy Smith's work is a combination of illustration and typography with a potentially humorous, energetic and optimistic atmosphere.

The exposition designs *Sunny Side Up* convey an idea of craftsmanship.

Cover and inside pages of the self-published promotional book *My Nose Smells Funny*.

Cinema Français is an illustration for the cover of the magazine *Sight and Sound*.

1. Design of illustration for a shirt with the phrase *Stitch your way to success*.

2. Poster designed to promote The Do Lectures, an organization that promotes the dissemination of ideas and knowledge. Limited Edition printed on recycled paper.

3. Illustration for an alternative invitation to one of the British royal weddings for the exhibition *HRHRSVP*.

4. Illustration for a University of the Arts London brochure.

Annelys de Vet

Amsterdam, the Netherlands
www.annelysdevet.nl

Annelys de Vet (1974) is a graphic designer and head of the design
department of the Sandberg Insti-
tuut Amsterdam (Masters Rietveld
Academie). Her work explores the role
of design in relation to the public and
political discourse. She earned her
BFA in 1997 at the HKU (NL), MFA in
1999 at the Sandberg Institute (NL)
and studied Sculpture at the RMIT,
Melbourne (1999-2000). Since 1997,
she runs her own studio, which has
have evolved from working for clients
such as Droog Design, Stedelijk Museum and KPN, to a more self-directed
practice where De Vet has published
several books concerning the representation of cultural and national
identity: *Subjectieve Atlas van Neder-
land* (BIS publishers, 2005), *The public role of the graphic designer* (Design
Academy Eindhoven, 2006), *Subjective
Atlas of Palestine* (010 Publishers,
2007) or *Subjective Atlas of Serbia*
(Dom Omladine, 2009).

This design consists of a calendar for the Puttershoek neighborhood. Each month words were selected related to the town's history and they were used in dish towels that were given as welcome gifts to new neighbors.

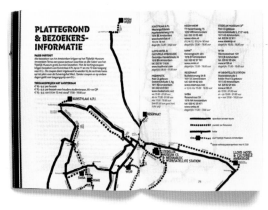

Artwork and guide for the temporary museum held in Tijdelijk Museum Amsterdam in collaboration with Rianne Petter in 2008. The temporary museum was a parallel program to the Amsterdam Art Fair between 2006 and 2009.

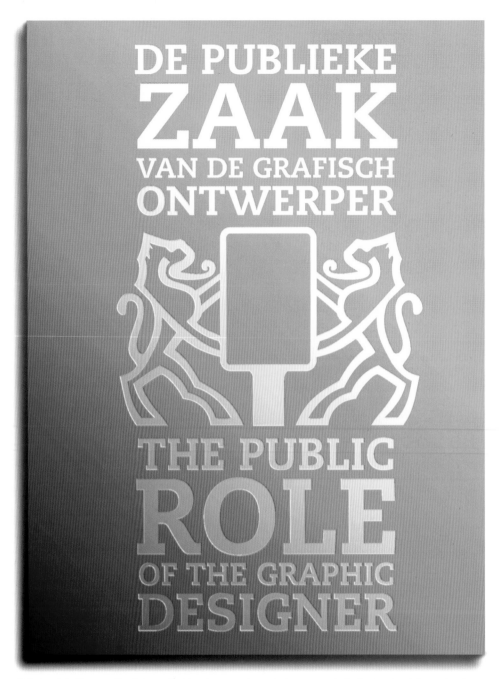

DE PUBLIEKE ZAAK VAN DE GRAFISCH ONTWERPER

THE PUBLIC ROLE OF THE GRAPHIC DESIGNER

This book is the result of the reflection from various designers and students about the role of graphic design in the creation of national symbols. Annelys de Vet coordinates the publication of this volume of 80 pages.

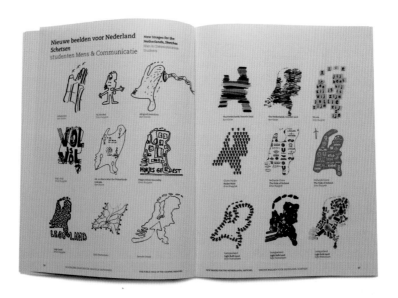

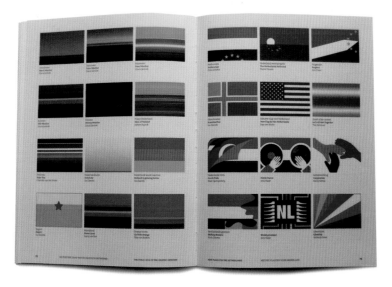

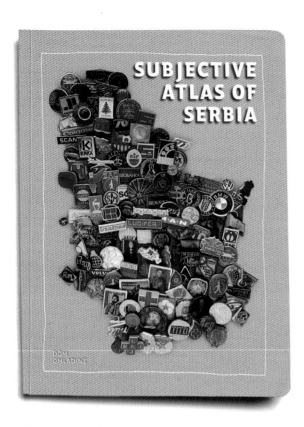

The subjective atlases dismantle the preconceived ideas of some countries, usually created from what appears in the media. The designer invited artists, photographers and designers to show their country as they see it.

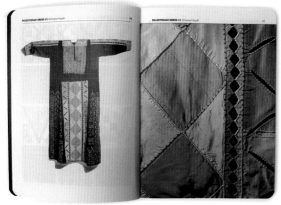

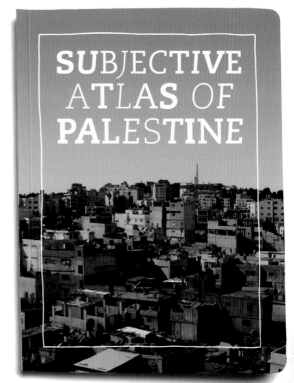

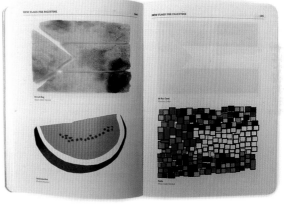

Ariane Spanier

Berlin, Germany
www.arianespanier.com

I was born in Weimar in 1978. I studied Visual Communication at the School
of Art and Design Berlin Weißensee.
After working at Sagmeister.Inc in
New York, I am running my design
studio ever since my return to Berlin
in 2005. My studio works with clients
from a cultural background, such as
galleries, publishers, architects and
museums. We create the design of
all sorts of printed forms, especially
for books, catalogs, posters, but also
corporate identities, logos, animations and websites. My clients include
the ETH Zürich, *The New York Times
Magazine*, 0047 Oslo and *Fukt Magazine*. My work has received, on several
occasions, credit from the Type Directors Club New York and was awarded
with the Polish Prize for Design, Slas-
ka Rzecz in 2007. In 2011, I won the
competition for the Corporate Design
of the Kieler Woche 2012, an annual
sailing festival in Germany with a history based on design competition.

Design of a poster as a contribution to the auction
Beautifully Banal for the Type Director's Club of New
York. Several designers were asked to adapt a local
newspaper ad.

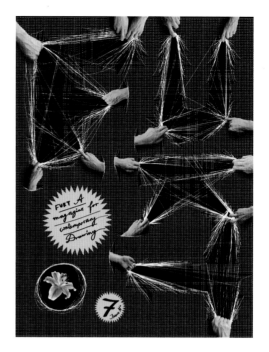

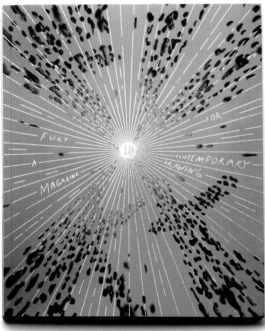

Design of several magazine covers for *Fukt*, contemporary drawing publication. Each number changes the layout and format.

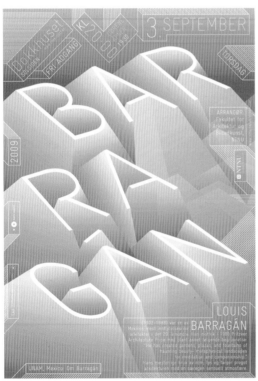

Design of a series of posters of a series of conferences organized by the University of Trondheim and given by renowned international architects such as Snøhetta, Barragan or Herreros/Lund.

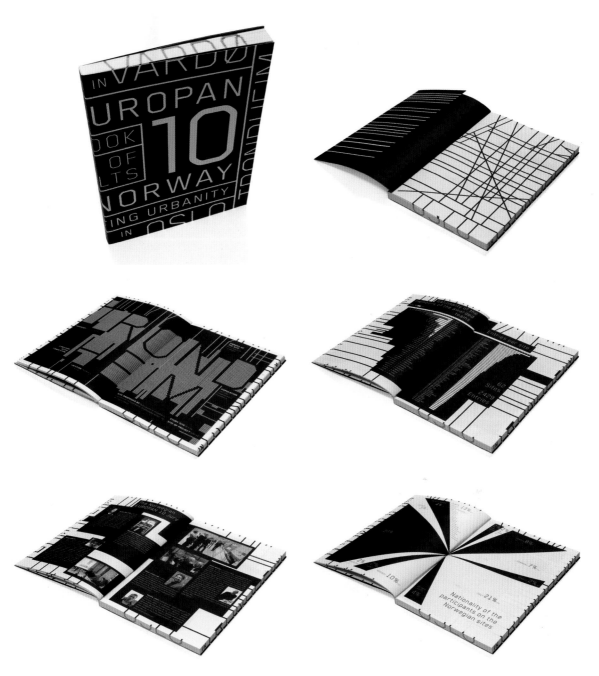

Brochure design with the results of the 10th edition of the Architecture Competition Europan Norway 2010.

Design of a double-sided poster-invitation of a facility for artists Björn Hegardt and Theo Ågren in Oslo.

Poster for one of the seminars given by designer Karin Sander in 2010.

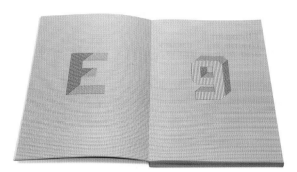

Catalog of Architecture Competition Europan Norway 2008. The theme of this edition was "Sustainable City and Public Spaces."

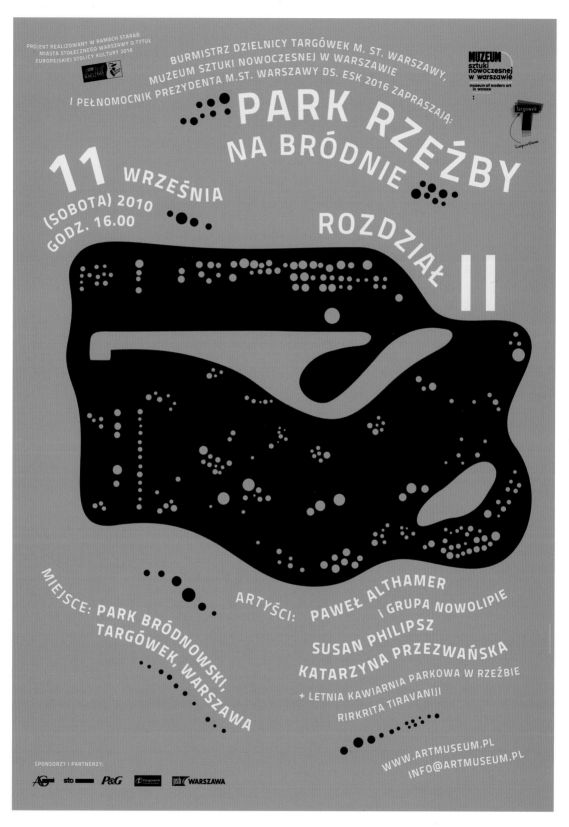

Design of a poster to promote the *2nd Chapter of the Bródno Sculpture Park*, a project developed by the Museum of Contemporary Art in Warsaw, Poland.

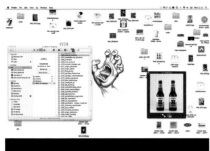

A-Side

Falmouth, UK
www.a-sidestudio.co.uk

We are A-Side: a full service creative studio established in the UK with a global reach. We offer bespoke design solutions spanning all media; we create and nurture successful brands, we offer art direction, graphic design and illustration all the while freely jumping the divides between image and product, design and art, the flat page and the moving image. We work collaboratively with our clients. Providing a flexible service, we prioritize our client's wishes, to help realize their vision and ensure mutually successful solutions. We are committed to producing design of the highest quality and our work reflects our ethos—accessible, human, and crafted.

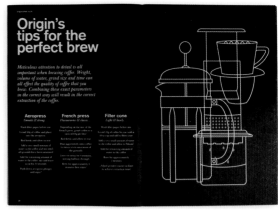

Development of the brand image of Origin Coffee
Roasters since its inception. Recent collaborations
include the 2011 catalog and the labels for the coffee
packages, designed by a few carefully selected artists.

YOUNG & NORGATE

MADE IN DEVON

Catalog and image of Young and Norgate, a group of designers and artisans who manufacture unique and elegant furniture. They are located in Devon and they have chosen the fox as the brand image to identify with the rural environment.

Poster for the 2011 edition of the Port Elliot's Festival. In collaboration with the renowned illustrator Ralph Steadman.

Design of labels, packaging and illustrations for the British clothing label Last & True.

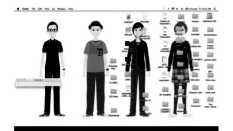

Asylum

Singapore, Singapore
www.theasylum.com.sg

I am the founder and Creative Director of Asylum, a creative company based in Singapore. Since our inception in 1999, we have worked on cross-disciplinary projects that include interactive design, environmental & interior design, packaging, branding and graphic design. Some of our projects include creating the Johnny Walker House in Shanghai, fashion accessories for Comme Des Garçons and the interior of Wanderlust Hotel. Featured in more than 30 international magazines from around the world, Asylum is defined as an unconventional maverick in the creative world. Other than the design studio, we have created our own retail store, curated exhibitions and even organized a concert for experimental music!

Asylum designed canvas bags and a few pins for Comme des Garcons inspired by the innocence of children and the non-conformist philosophy of the label.

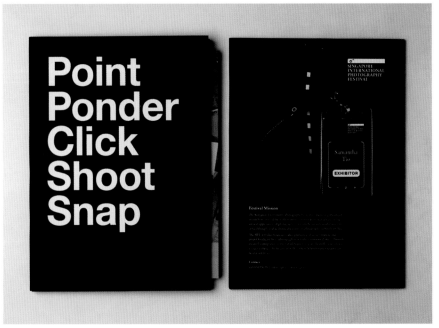

Image for the International Photography Festival of Singapore, biennial meeting whose main objective is to publicize the advances in photography.

1. Packaging design of cocktail-flavored chocolates, including Tequila Sunrise to Whisky on the Rocks. The pattern on the package is based on the liquor brands used in the cocktails.

2-3. Design for Tanjong Beach Club, Singapore. The image of a swimmer has been used.

Catalog of the works of moviemaker Ho Tzu Nyen, selected to represent Singapore at the 54th Venice Biennale.

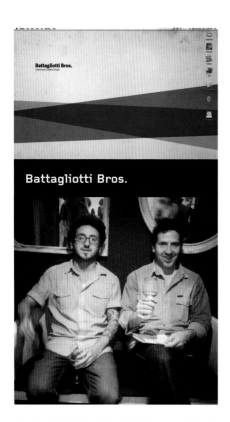

Battagliotti Bros.

Barcelona, Spain
www.battagliottibros.com

We are a graphic design studio specializing in *licensing design*, a concept
that seeks graphical extension of the
brand, with the intention of exporting
it to other products. We create tools so
that this added value goes beyond the
aesthetic. We design beginning with
the creation of the style guide and
product development to implementation at the point of sale. Pilo and Viru
are two brothers with a single goal: to
seriously make a business fun.

Pilo and Viru's work in the field of style guides can be seen in this series
of graphics applications for the Futbol Club Barcelona.

Blaugrana al vent
un crit valent
tenim un nom
el sap tothom:

BARÇA! BARÇA! BARÇA!

These retro designs include covers, icons, packaging and graphics applications.

Scalextric

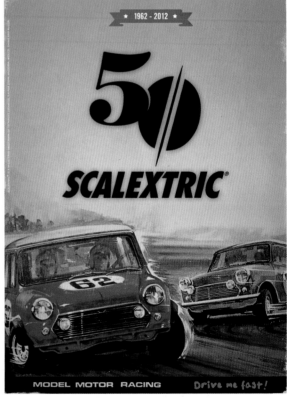

Scalextric is a well known brand of miniature cars with electric drive. These designs were created for the style guide of the brand and include a 50th anniversary logo, icons and graphics applications for the brand products.

Design of a poster for the Tour de France, in which the yellow is the prominent color, the color of the jersey of the winner.

JUEVES 17 DE JUNIO / 22:30 hs

NUEVO DISCO
WWW.AUSTRIABAND.COM

Design of concert posters and launch of the new album
by the Argentine Group Austria.

AUSTRIA

JUEVES 27 MAYO / 21:30
SAINTS BAR / LAVALLE 4082
PALERMO / CAPITAL / BS AS
/WWW.MYSPACE.COM/AUSTRIASPACE

Design of two posters and a CD cover for McNamara, a
bar-restaurant with live music in Rosario, Argentina.

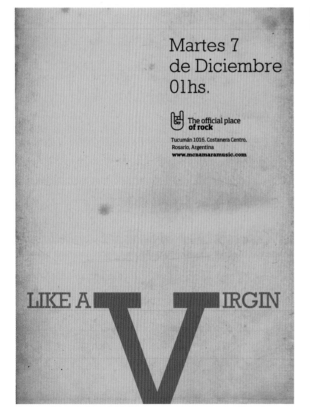

Poster for the festival of La Dreta de l'Eixample, a district in Barcelona.

Begson

Reno, NV, USA
www.begson.com

My name is Craig Holden Feinberg. I was born in 1980 and spent most of my childhood in Columbia, Maryland USA. I received my BFA in graphic design from The University of the Arts in Philadelphia, Pennsylvania, where I was awarded the Thesis Citation and Faculty Award. Intent on furthering my design experience, I was accepted at Fabrica, The United Colors of Benetton Communications Research and Development Center in Treviso, Italy. I have been published in magazines such as *Colors*, *Vorn*, and *Fab*. I've worked closely with the World Health Organization, International Council of Nurses and Fabrica Features, among others. I have been published in *Contemporary Graphic Design* by Taschen.

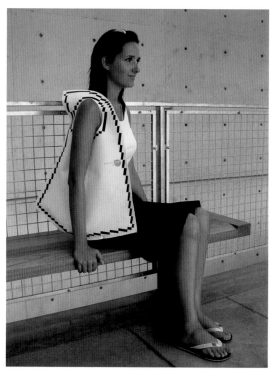

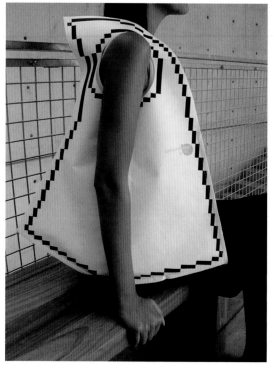

Design of a bag in collaboration with Krv Kurva Design, a Portuguese studio for a dam rehabilitation program. The fabric is Tyvek®.

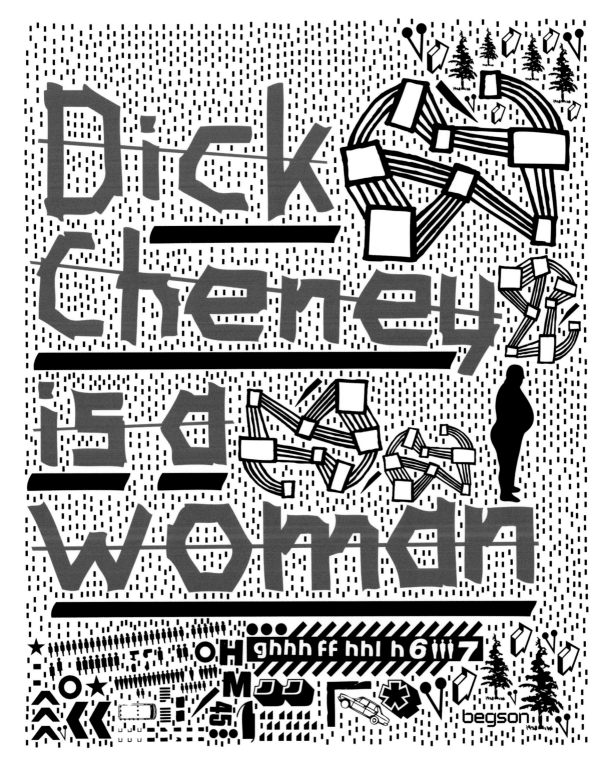

The work *Dick Cheney Is A Woman* was created for a group exhibition for the gallery Illiterate. It was carried out by hand with two CMYK colors, black and magenta.

1

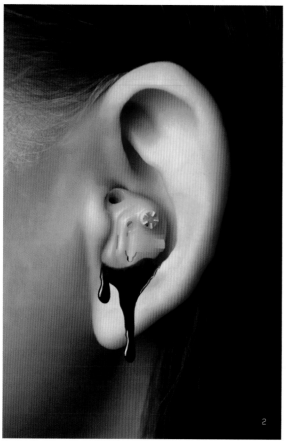

2

1. Paper design which pays homage to the Letraset system, which represented a revolution in graphic design.

2. Poster against domestic and sexual violence on deaf people, especially women and children.

THE LITTLE BOOK
OF SHOCKING
FOOD FACTS

CRAIG HOLDEN FEINBERG & DALE PETERSEN

The Little Book of Shocking Food Facts is a project carried out by Charlotte and Peter Fiell, former Taschen design editors. This volume was presented at the London Book Fair.

THERE ARE CURRENTLY 923 MILLION
STARVING PEOPLE IN THE WORLD.
FOOD AND AGRICULTURE ORGANIZATION OF THE UNITED NATIONS (FAO), 2008

BASED ON CURRENT TRENDS,
THE GLOBAL FISHING INDUSTRY
WILL BE IN A STATE OF COMPLETE
COLLAPSE BY 2048.
SCIENCE, 2006

THE INTENSIVE RAISING OF CHICKENS IS
ASSOCIATED WITH MANY SERIOUS WELFARE
CONCERNS SUCH AS EXTREMELY HIGH
STOCKING DENSITIES, FEED RESTRICTION,
BEAK TRIMMING AND FORCED MOULTING.
ANIMAL SCIENCE DEPARTMENT ULUDAĞ UNIVERSITY, TURKEY, 2006

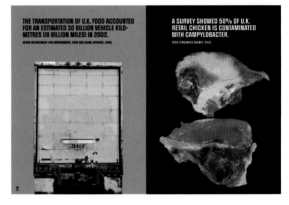

THE TRANSPORTATION OF U.K. FOOD ACCOUNTED
FOR AN ESTIMATED 30 BILLION VEHICLE KILO-
METRES (19 BILLION MILES) IN 2002.
DEFRA (DEPARTMENT FOR ENVIRONMENT, FOOD AND RURAL AFFAIRS), 2006

A SURVEY SHOWED 50% OF U.K.
RETAIL CHICKEN IS CONTAMINATED
WITH CAMPYLOBACTER.
FOOD STANDARDS AGENCY, 2003

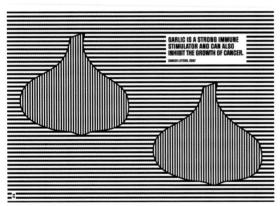

GARLIC IS A STRONG IMMUNE
STIMULATOR AND CAN ALSO
INHIBIT THE GROWTH OF CANCER.
CANCER LETTERS, 2007

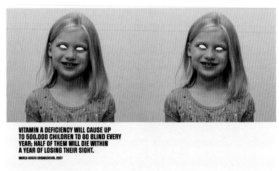

VITAMIN A DEFICIENCY WILL CAUSE UP
TO 500,000 CHILDREN TO GO BLIND EVERY
YEAR; HALF OF THEM WILL DIE WITHIN
A YEAR OF LOSING THEIR SIGHT.
WORLD HEALTH ORGANIZATION, 2007

This book combines provocative images with startling
facts about food policy, food production, etc. The goal is
to make the reader think about their eating habits.

CHINESE MEAT CONSUMPTION PER PERSON HAS MORE THAN DOUBLED SINCE 1995, FROM 25 KG (55 LB) PER PERSON TO 53 KG (117 LB).

BIOFUELS DIGEST, 2008

THE ANTIOXIDANTS THAT ARE ABUNDANT IN FRUITS, VEGETABLES AND TEA ARE VALUABLE TO US BECAUSE THEY PROVIDE A LONGER LIFE, REDUCED CANCER RISK, AND LOWER THE INCIDENCE OF CARDIO-VASCULAR DISEASE.

BRITISH FOOD JOURNAL, 1996

A REDUCTION IN THE MINERAL CONTENT OF FRUITS AND VEGETABLES HAS BEEN SEEN OVER TIME IN THE U.K., WITH DECLINES OF UP TO 80%.

BRITISH FOOD JOURNAL, 1997

THE GULF OF MEXICO CONTAINS AN AREA OF UP TO 20,000 KM² (THE SIZE OF NEW JERSEY) REFERRED TO AS A DEAD ZONE—SO CALLED BECAUSE NOTHING CAN LIVE THERE DUE TO THE OXYGEN-DEPLETION CAUSED BY FERTILISER RUN-OFF.

JOURNAL OF ENVIRONMENTAL QUALITY, 2001

PHTHALATES ARE CHEMICALS, USED IN CONSUMER PRODUCTS AND FOOD PACKAGING, WHICH FIND THEIR WAY INTO FOODS SUCH AS INFANT FORMULA AND BABY FOOD AND ARE KNOWN TO DISRUPT REPRODUCTIVE DEVELOPMENT.

TOXICOLOGICAL SCIENCES, 2000

Ben Faydherbe

The Hague, the Netherlands
www.ben-wout.nl

I am a graphic designer from The Hague, born in Amsterdam in 1958. In 1986, after my training at the Royal Academy of Arts in The Hague, and several years of work at Vorm Vijf, I started my studio with Wout de Vringer. We specialised in work for theater, film and art. Today my work depends largely on assignments in the public and cultural sector. In 2002, I became member of the AGI. I am closely involved with Ruimtevaart Foundation's activities; in particular it's style of houses and communication. In the designs I try to work with the final event in mind, it doesn't necessarily have to be a direct translation of it.

Ground Three / Full Screen exhibition poster in the Ruimtevaart Foundation in 2008.

Ground Two / DIY exhibition. Design of poster and wall with photographs of Ruimtevaart Foundation building in 2007.

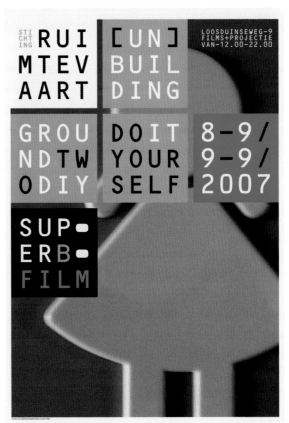

The design of posters stands out among Ben Faydherbe's work. Here are the posters of the exhibition *Ex-Mêkh Takes Five*, an exhibit in which the works of different artists is presented every week.

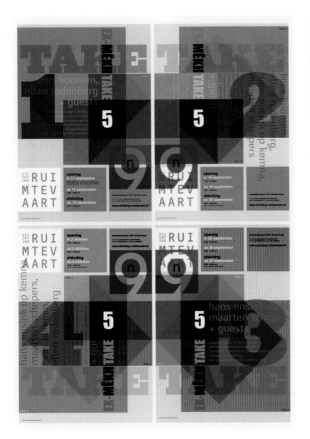

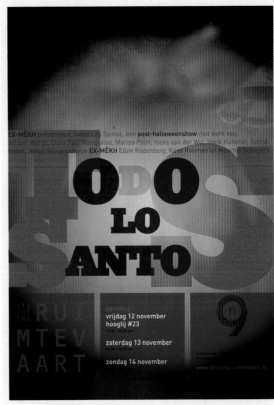

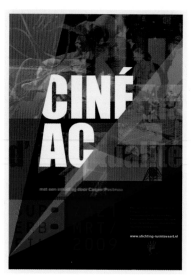

These posters were designed for the program *Super B*, a cycle of movies with different themes: jazz, joy of life, etc.

DE
49
(50–1)
STOELEN
VAN
VAN AGT

SEX

SUP-
ERB-
FILM

ZA30
OKT/
2010

zaal open 20.00 uur | aanvang 21.00 uur
toegang 5 euro
loosduinseweg 9 | 2571 AA den haag

samenstelling | josé de bruin | henk
hubenet | barney de krijger | willem marijs |
albert wulffers

informatie | info@stichting-ruimtevaart.nl

www.stichting-ruimtevaart.nl

Bendertainment
(Mario Bender)

Berlin, Germany
www.bendertainment.com

I am a freelance web and graphic designer based in Berlin, specialized in building custom web and print design, logo and apparel design. After working for a popular streetwear label, I started up my own business called Bendertainment. I love taking on challenges and seizing the chance to push my skills to a higher ground. When I'm not sitting behind my desk, you can find me making my six string Paula scream... Hell Yeah!

Several t-shirt designs made for several labels, including
the German Iriedaily.

Poster of the German punk band born in the 90's The Crack Whore Society.

Poster of a concert by The Ting Tings in Hamburg, within the *Myspace Secret Shows*.

Bendita Gloria

Barcelona, Spain
www.benditagloria.com

Bendita Gloria is a design studio formed by Alba Rosell and Santi Fuster. With a background in graphic design and graphic arts, we decided to start our own project in 2007. Today we can say we have experience in identity, publishing and packaging ... but we no longer believe in these labels. We have a special interest in printed artwork and uphold our approach to design projects from the concept. We are agnostic. We´ll see you in the glory.

are YOU scared of making money?

☐ yes ☑ no

are YOU gonna sign the agreement?

☑ yes ☐ no

Impress the ladies, amaze your friends, and prove to your business associates that you have arrived on luxury and class for just 2€ per month.

How I became a financial product

by Rafel Oliva

"a Royal win-win deal"

Rafael Oliva is funding a master at the Royal College of Arts in London with the sale of shares of what will be his professional career after completing his studies.

GUANYA OR ENJOIA'T 2011

PREMIS DE JOIERIA CONTEMPORÀNIA
PREMIOS DE JOYERÍA CONTEMPORÁNEA
CONTEMPORARY JEWELRY AWARDS

15 / 9   Entrada lliure   20h

GUANYA 15 / 9 OR 20h ENJOIA'T 2011

PREMIS DE JOIERIA CONTEMPORÀNIA

PREMIOS DE JOYERÍA CONTEMPORÁNEA

CONTEMPORARY JEWELRY AWARDS

Entrada lliure

GUANYA OR

ENJOIA'T 2011

PREMIS DE JOIERIA CONTEMPORÀNIA

PREMIOS DE JOYERÍA CONTEMPORÁNEA

CONTEMPORARY JEWELRY AWARDS

15 / 9 - 20h
Entrada lliure

15 / 9   20h

ENJOIA'T 2011

PREMIS DE JOIERIA CONTEMPORÀNIA • PREMIOS DE JOYERÍA CONTEMPORÁNEA • CONTEMPORARY JEWELRY AWARDS

Entrada lliure

GUANYA OR

Contemporary jewelry prizes awards Enjoia't reward the ability to challenge the limits of jewelry. The artwork adopts the style of jewelry pawn shops that drew attention to the cry of "buy gold" in this case "win gold."

YES
WE
WINE

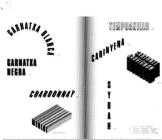
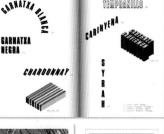

CHEERS!

Casa Mariol is a family of winegrowers from Terra Alta, proud of their land and their agricultural model. They concluded that the luxury that often goes hand in hand with bottles of wine is not them. Thus, the wines are named with their variety and age.

We are Desigual is the code of conduct from the known fashion company Desigual. The publication takes the form of a Bible imbued in the style of the brand.

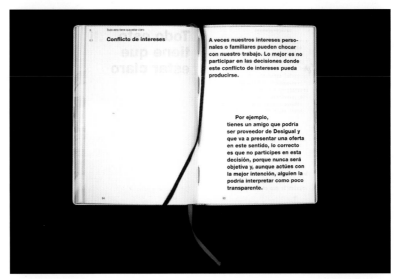

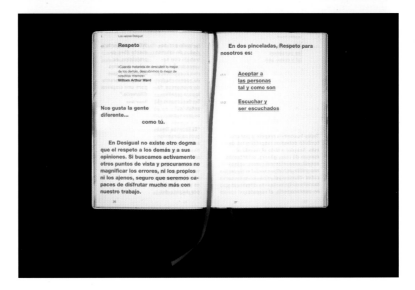

Blokdesign

Toronto, Canada
www.blokdesign.com

Blok is a design studio specializing in brand identities and experiences, packaging, exhibit design, installations and editorial design. We also design and publish books and have produced a line of dishware. Now here's what we REALLY do: submerge ourselves in the world around us, seek out the normal, the abnormal, the mundane, the exciting, the current, the obsolete, the real, the fake, the inspiring, the disheartening, and then use what we see to find surprising, compelling ways to move people. And we do it by collaborating with highly talented thinkers from around the world, taking on initiatives that blend cultural awareness, a love of art and humanity to advance society and business alike.

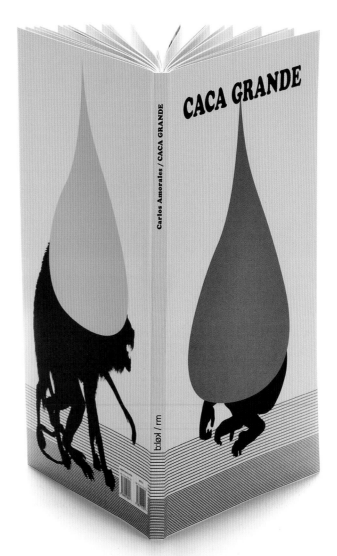

First volume in a series of children's books designed to stimulate the children's imagination. Each book is a collaboration with a contemporary artist.

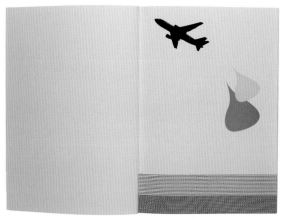

Caca Grande is the work of the Mexican artist Carlos Amorales.

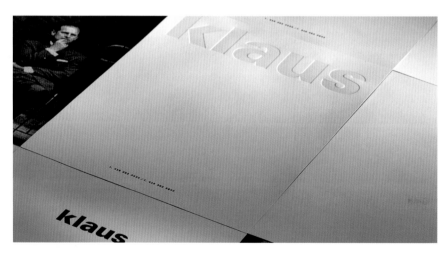

Design of the corporate identity of the furniture company Klaus. The elegance, modernity and timelessness of the brand was made stand out.

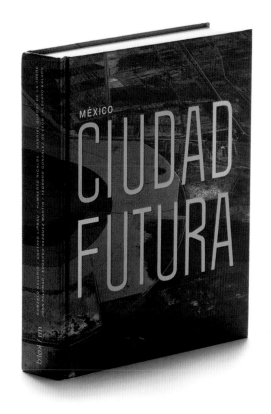

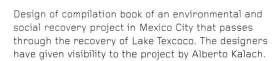

VIVIENDAS 3.8 millones/ÁREAS NATURALES PROTEGIDAS 1 319.06km²/ÁREA DE CUENCA 9 726 km² / POBLACIÓN 19 239.910 habitantes CALIDAD DEL AIRE 80% del año no es satisfactoria ÁREAS VERDES 1.94m² por hab/ÁREAS EROSIONADAS 32 000 hectáreas erosionadas/ÁREAS DEFORESTADAS 32% del territorio/RESIDUOS SÓLIDOS 1.17 kilogramos al día por habitante. 2010

Design of compilation book of an environmental and social recovery project in Mexico City that passes through the recovery of Lake Texcoco. The designers have given visibility to the project by Alberto Kalach.

RADIOGRAFÍAS DE LA CUENCA DE MÉXICO

SON UNA SERIE DE PLANOS DE LA CIUDAD DE MÉXICO QUE, DESDE EL MISMO ENCUADRE Y A LA MISMA ESCALA, MUESTRAN SUS CONDICIONES NATURALES Y LA MODIFICACIÓN DEL PAISAJE HECHA POR EL HOMBRE A LO LARGO DEL TIEMPO (URBANIZACIÓN, CULTIVOS, CANALES, CAMINOS, DRENAJES, PARQUES Y DEFORESTACIÓN).

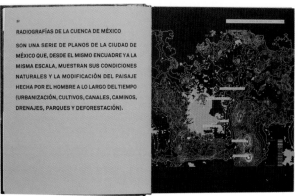

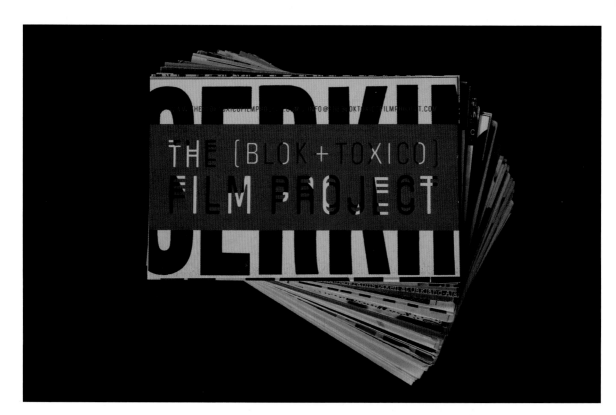

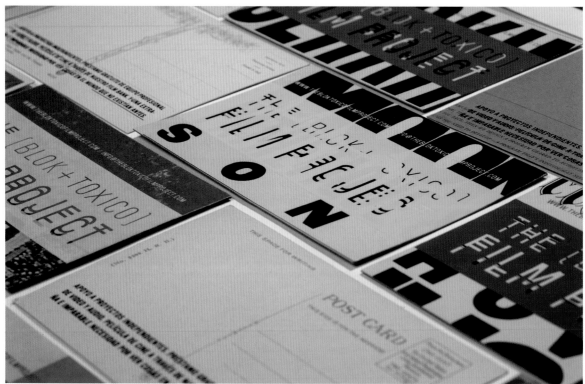

Image and logo design of *Film Project*, a project assisting the development and filming of movies. This project is a collaboration between Blockdesign and Toxic, an independent cultural studies center.

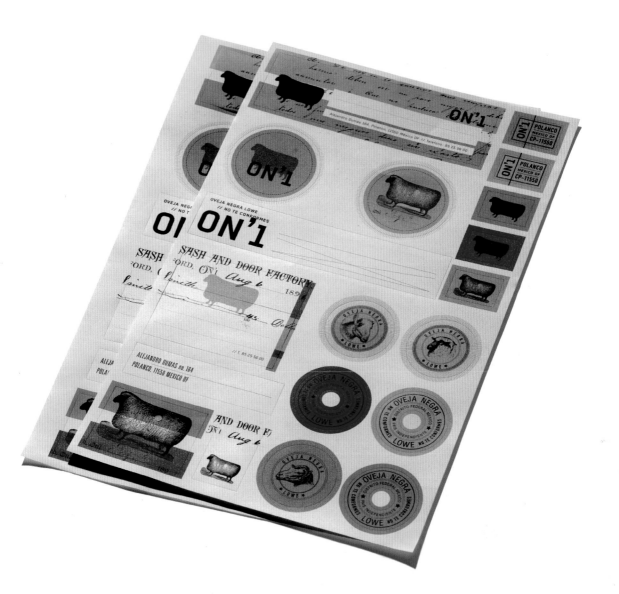

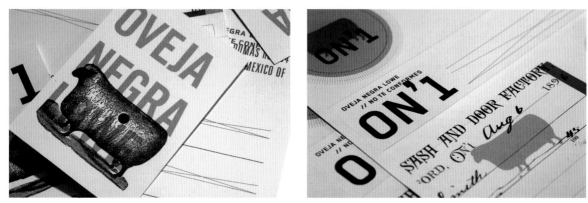

The design of the image of two companies that came together, one international and the other local, represented a challenge for designers, who created an acronym for the two companies to represent the union.

Boy Bastiaens

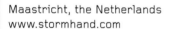

Maastricht, the Netherlands
www.stormhand.com

Working from my studio in the southern part of the Netherlands, I design for commercial and cultural clients on a variety of national and international projects. A majority of my assignments are branding and identity related. My work covers the fields of graphic design, art direction, illustration, packaging, product design and new media, allowing me to design on a multidisciplinary level. Quite some time in the studio is dedicated to experimenting and trying to break away from standards and routine.

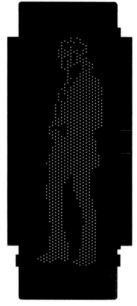

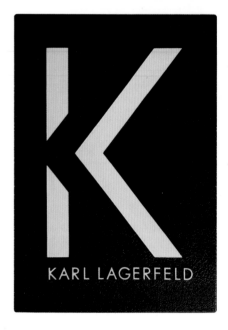

Selection of graphic elements for the fashion label K by Karl Lagerfeld. This project was developed with great attention to detail, such as the design of the pixilated silhouette, and the innovative use of materials.

KARL LAGERFELD

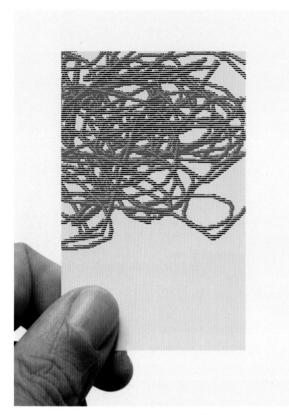

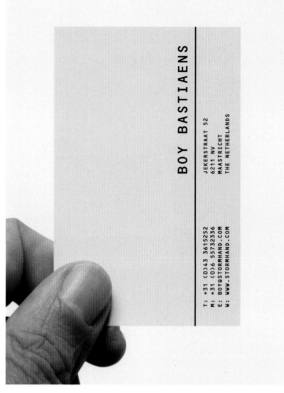

BOY BASTIAENS

JEKERSTRAAT 52
6211 NV
MAASTRICHT
THE NETHERLANDS

T: +31 (0)43 3615252
M: +31 (0)6 55732336
E: BOY@STORMHAND.COM
W: WWW.STORMHAND.COM

Designers own corporate image: business cards, CDs and cases. The design uses abstract lines and images as a starting point that symbolizes the essence of graphic design projects.

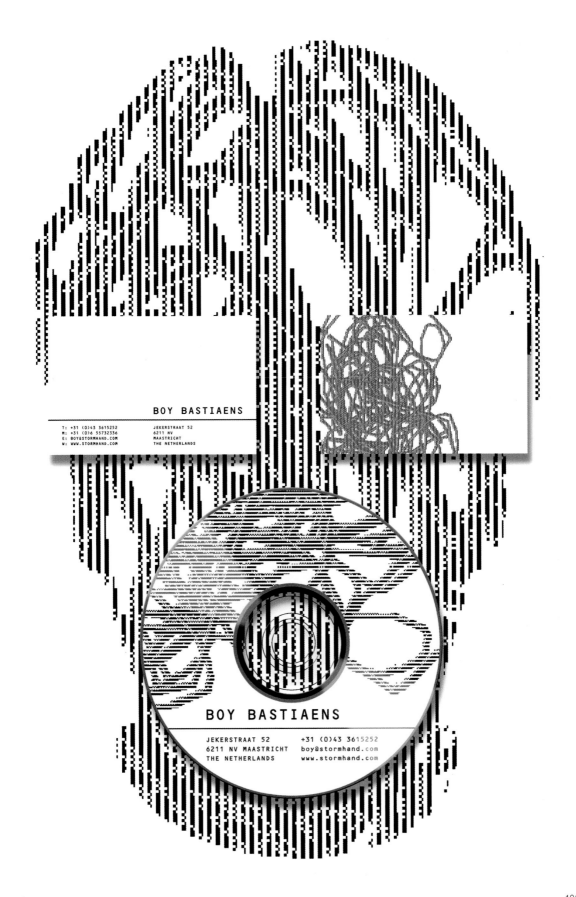

BOY BASTIAENS

T: +31 (0)43 3615252
M: +31 (0)6 55732336
E: BOY@STORMHAND.COM
W: WWW.STORMHAND.COM

JEKERSTRAAT 52
6211 NV
MAASTRICHT
THE NETHERLANDS

BOY BASTIAENS

JEKERSTRAAT 52   +31 (0)43 3615252
6211 NV MAASTRICHT   boy@stormhand.com
THE NETHERLANDS   www.stormhand.com

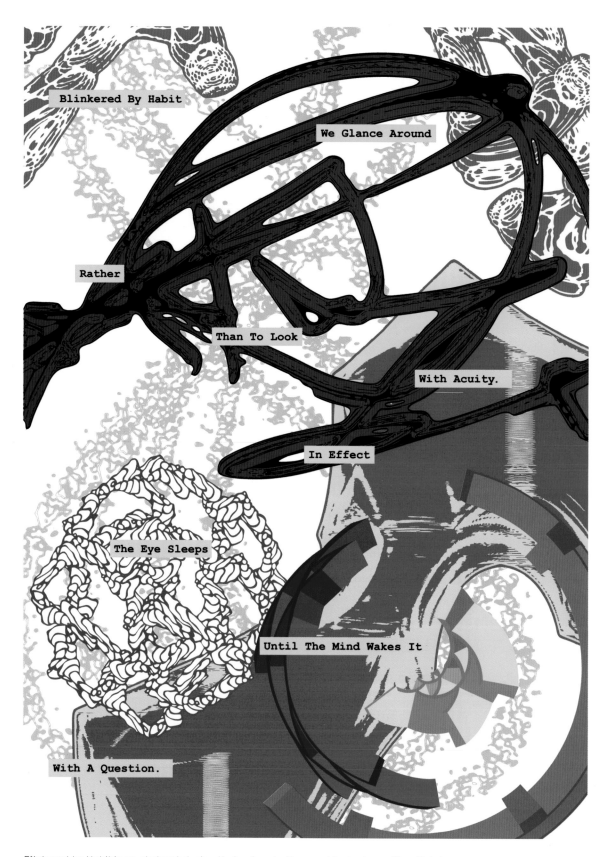

Blinkered By Habit

We Glance Around

Rather

Than To Look

With Acuity.

In Effect

The Eye Sleeps

Until The Mind Wakes It

With A Question.

Blinkered by Habit is an abstract design that refers to the graphic designer Alan Fletcher.

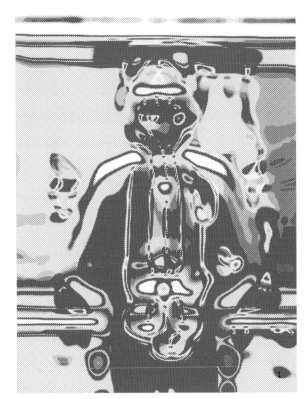

1. *Airfellow* is a personal project, a styling exercise based on the use of frames.

2. Next *Im Dschungel Des Geschmacks* is a personal project, an exercise of accidental poetry, where it plays with the idea of aesthetic criteria from an unconventional process based on coincidence.

Bruketa&Žinić OM

BRUKETA&ŽINIĆ OM

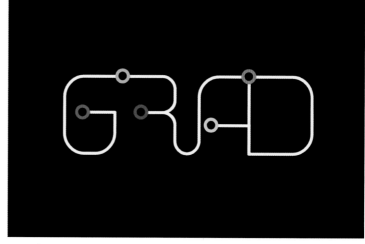

Zagreb, Croatia
www.bruketa-zinic.com

Our agency is called Bruketa&Žinić OM and it consists of advertising agencies Bruketa&Žinić OM Zagreb, Bruketa&Žinić OM Baku, brand consultants Brandoctor and digital agency Brlog and Brigada, adesign studio specialized in optimization of retail stores, product design and architecture. There's around 50 of us. We have won over 300 international awards for our work , such as the Art Directors Club New York, Epica, London International Awards, New York Festivals, Cresta, Clio, Effie, etc. You can learn more and read all about us on our blog at www.bruketa-zinic.com.

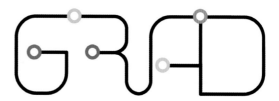

Grad (city in Serbia) is a cultural and debate center in Belgrade. The corporate image enhances the ideas of network communication, constant movement and a meeting point.

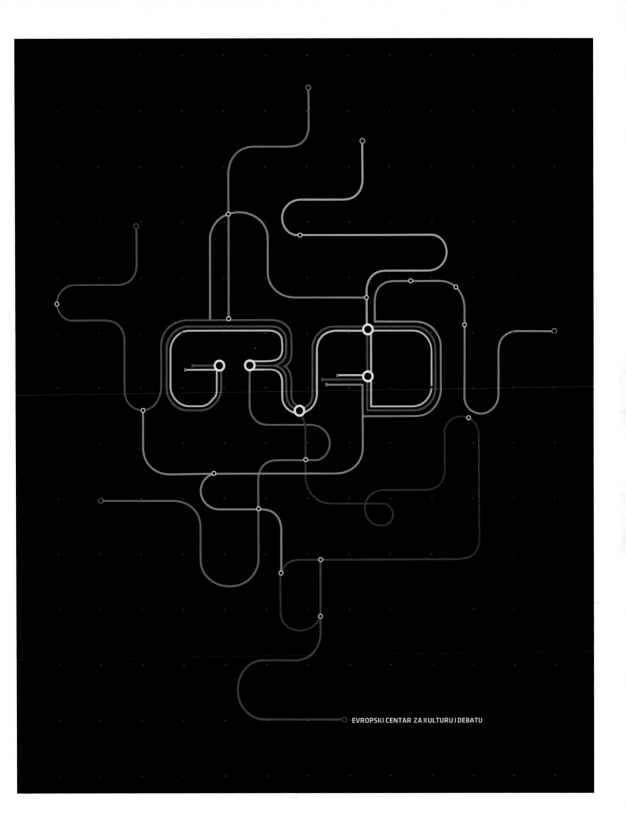

EVROPSKI CENTAR ZA KULTURU I DEBATU

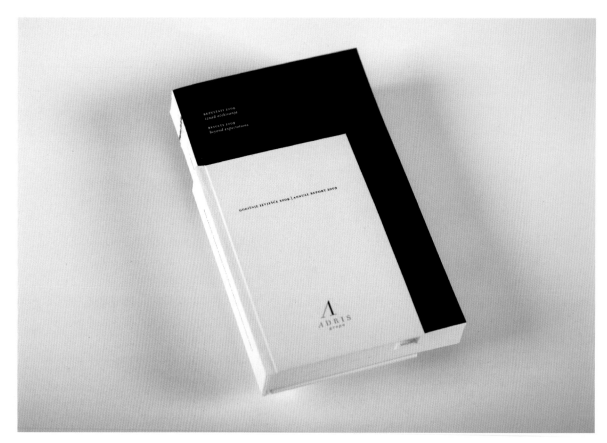

Beyond Expectations is the title that has been given to Adris Group's company annual report, a firm that, in spite of the crisis, has attained good results.

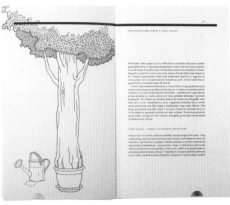

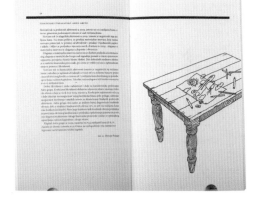

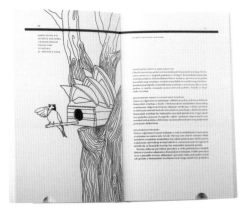

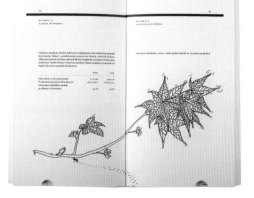

POLOVICA KOJA ČINI RAZLIKU.

50% kakao

božićna / rasprodaja

1. Television advertisement for Dorina Fifty, chocolate manufacturer with 50% cocoa, which is what stands out in the ad.

2. Poster for the Warehouse-sk8 holiday season, supplier of skateboarding material.

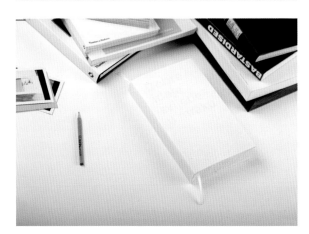

2008 Adris Group Annual Report. The project *Good Ideas Glow in the Dark* wants to emphasize that bright ideas help businesses succeed.

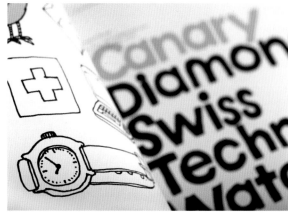

This book contains 52 pages of original artwork, all with spam as the main theme: advertising what their representative messages are and what spam will be like in the future.

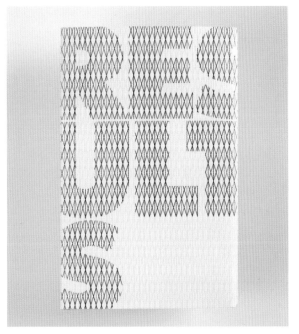
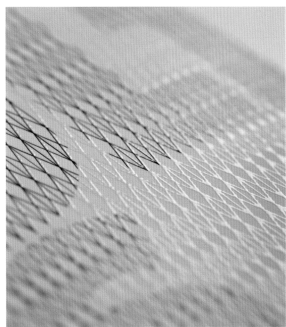

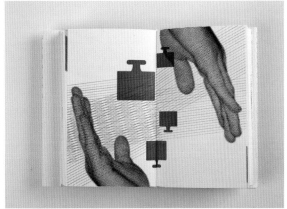

The 2010 Adris Group annual report emphasizes the results of the company and includes illustrations that refer to different business areas.

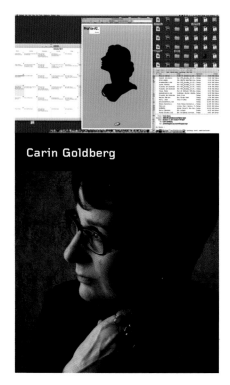

Carin Goldberg

New York, NY, USA
http://caringoldberg.com

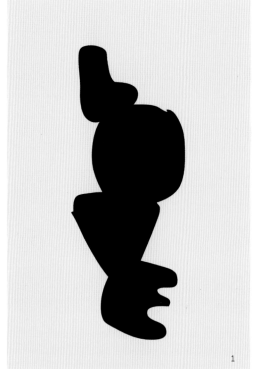

Carin Goldberg was born in New York City and studied at the Cooper Union School of Art. She began her career as a designer at CBS Television, CBS Records and Atlantic Records before establishing her own firm in 1982. Over the following two decades, Carin designed hundreds of book jackets for all the major American publishing houses, including Random House and Harper Collins, and dozens of album covers for record labels such as Warner Bros or Motown. The breadth of her work covers artists as diverse as Kurt Vonnegut and Susan Sontag, Dvorák and Madonna. Her book jacket for the 1986 reissue of James Joyce's *Ulysses* has become an icon of postmodern design. From 2003 to 2004 she was Creative Director at Time Inc. Custom Publishing. Her recent projects include design of the book *Last Letters Home: Voices of Americans from the Battlefields of Iraq* (Life Books, 2005) based on the HBO documentary.

1. Design of a banner to celebrate Valentine's Day, commissioned by Times Square Alliance.

2. Illustration for the exhibition *The Black Cube*, commissioned by the Art Directors Club.

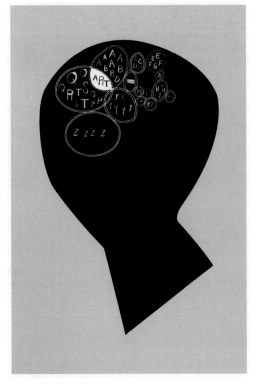

Alphabet Poster Series commissioned by a philanthropic institution.

Cover and interior illustrations of a report in 2010 of the *New York Times* on Kafka's unpublished letters.

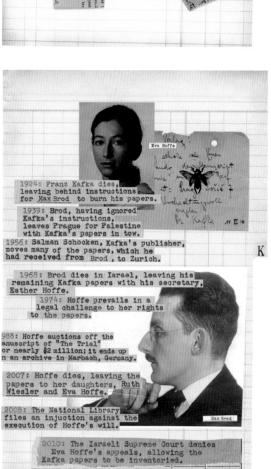

Design of a promotional poster for the School of Visual Arts in New York. The poster was displayed in the subway in New York between August and October 2010.

UN SEDICESIMO
CARIN GOLDBERG
NUMERO 14A
GENNAIO - FEBBRAIO
2010 REGISTRAZIONE AL
TRIBUNALE DI MANTOVA
N.1 DEL 03/02/2007
ISCRIZIONE AL ROC
N.15649 DEL 01/06/2007
DIRETTORE RESPONSABILE
FEDERICO MAGGIONI
PROGETTO A CURA DI
PIETRO CORRAINI
STAMPATO IN ITALIA DA
GRAFICHE SIZ, VERONA
© 2010 CARIN GOLDBERG
MAURIZIO CORRAINI S.R.L.
VIA IPPOLITO NIEVO
7A - 46100 MANTOVA
WWW.UNSEDICESIMO.COM
WWW.CORRAINI.COM
WWW.SIZ.COM ☐ 5 EURO

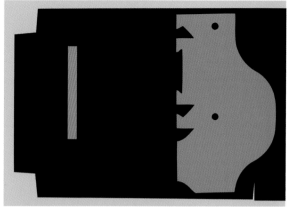

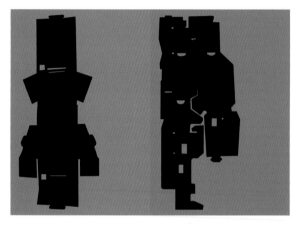

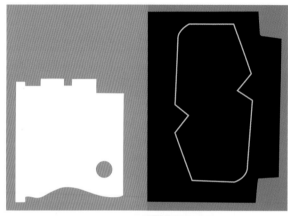

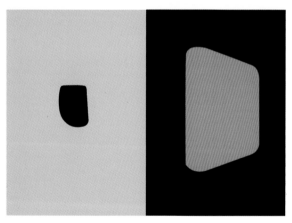

The publisher Corraini Editions regularly invites an artist to the 16-page monthly publication *Un Sedicesimo*. The design by Carin Goldberg is based on cut-out shapes and packing boxes.

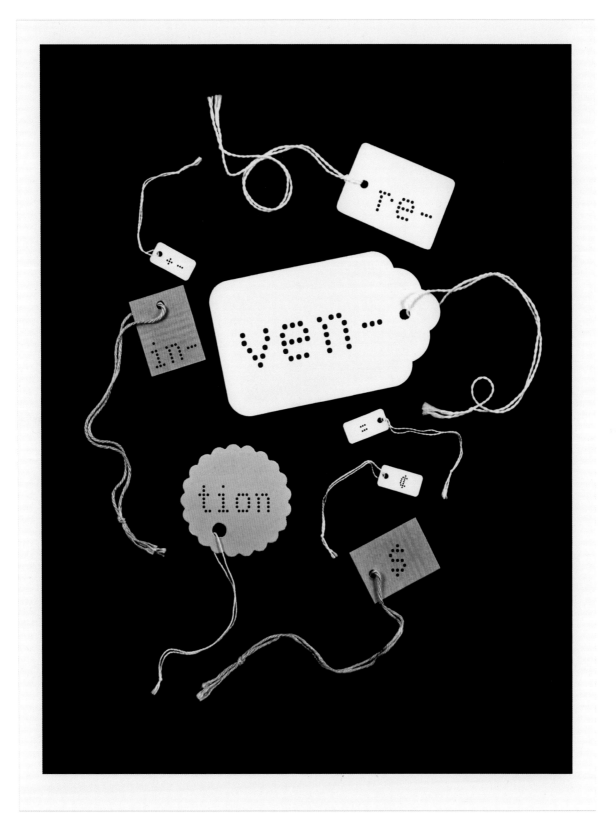

Reinvention poster. The tags are the title of the work.

Catalogtree

Arnhem, the Netherlands
www.catalogtree.net

We are a multidisciplinary design studio founded in 2001. The studio is based in Arnhem, the Netherlands and works continuously on commissioned and self-initiated design projects. Our guiding design tactic is *form=behaviour*. Typography, generative graphic design and the visualization of quantitative data are daily routines. Other recent endeavors include: D.I.Y. structured-light 3D-scanning and the visualization of financial tick-data. We recently built a crystal radio.

Illustrations made for the *New York Times*. The first, on the influence of social networks on obesity. The second accompanies a data visualization article.

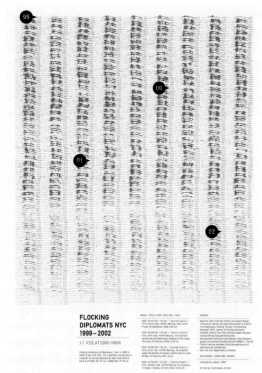

FD-3

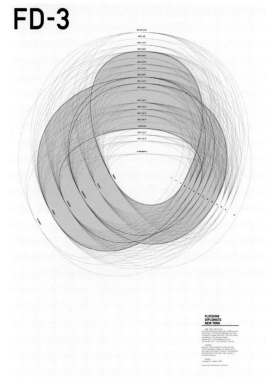

FD-5

These six screenprints show the data collected by scientists Ray Fisman and Edward Miguel on unpaid parking tickets by diplomats in New York.

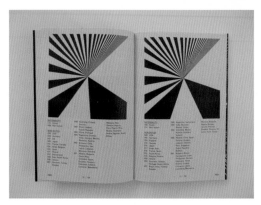
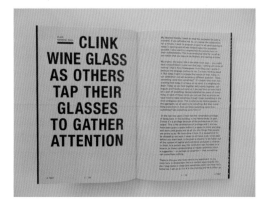

Design of catalog for the Atelier exhibition. The catalog shows the documentation of the work process of the artists and is also a showcase for the exhibited works.

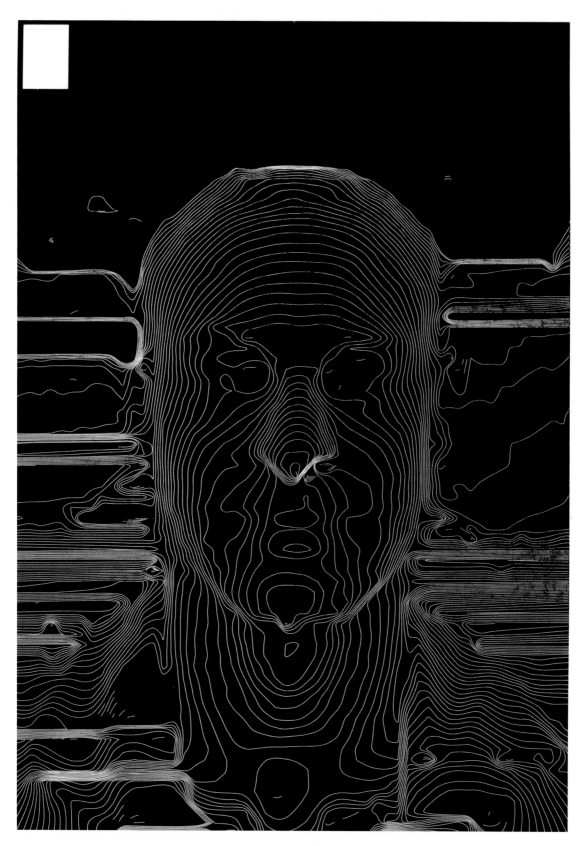

Relief printing of a portrait with a 3D scanner in which each of the coordinates, X, Y and Z were processed and visualized in different ways.

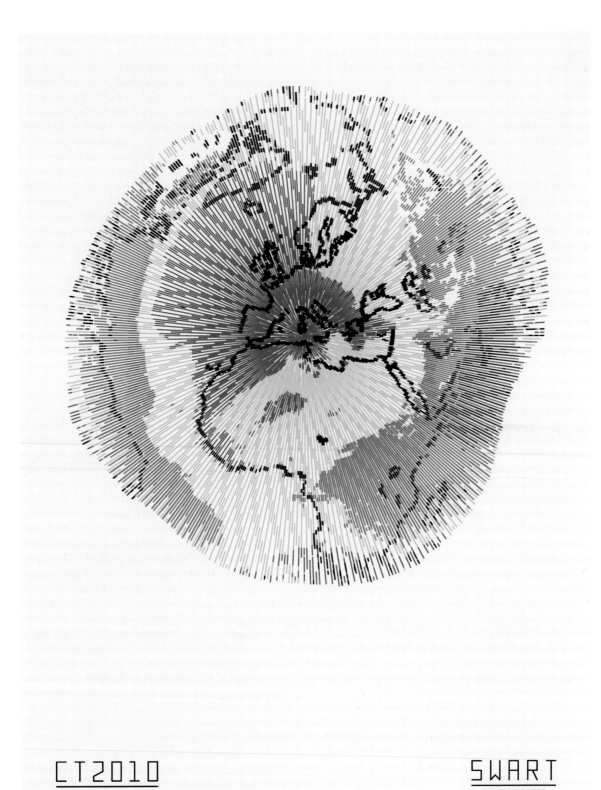

CT2010

SWART

EEN PASSIE VOOR
ZWAARTEKRACHT

Visualization of the fields of gravity on a drawing of the
land in CMYK carried out with plotter pencil.

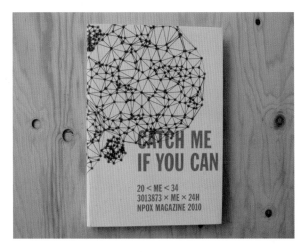
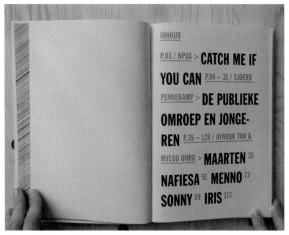
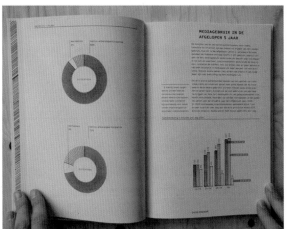
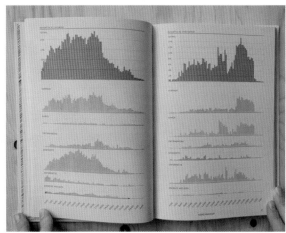
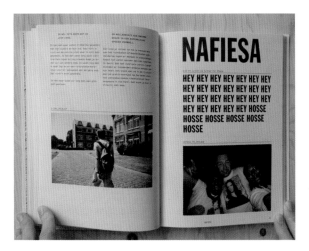

Design of magazine *Catch Me If You Can* for the NPOX10 festival. The computer graphics were done with pen plotter.

Chris Bolton

Anton&Anton

Helsinki, Finland
www.chrisbolton.org

Chris Bolton is a British/Canadian educated graphic designer, based in Helsinki. He is working on music, art, retail, fashion, architecture, advertising and publishing projects worldwide. His thought-provoking work delivers a clear and relevant result, regardless of scale or budget. Recent clients include Marimekko, Nokia, Levis, Kiasma Contemporary Art Museum, Skanno and Eskimo Recordings. He has also worked with Comme Des Garçons, Escalator Records and A-Lehdet to mention a few.

Corporate Image Design for Anton & Anton, an organic food store.

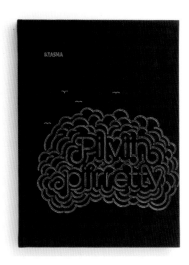

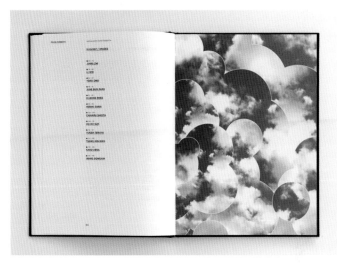

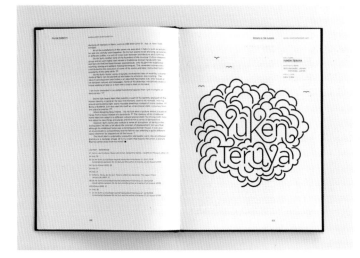

Designing a typeface for the catalog of an exhibition commissioned by the Museum of Contemporary Art in Kiasma. The font displays the names of the artists in the exhibition *Drawn in the Clouds*.

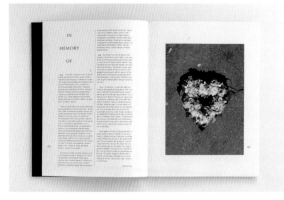

Design of book-catalog of the exhibition *In Memory of*, by
the artist Heta Kuchka, on death and funerals.

JANNE RÄISÄNEN 07.02 - 02.03.2008

Collaboration with the artist Janne Raisin for creating illustrations for her catalog.

YOURS TRULY

Heta Kuchka 6.10. – 10.12.2006

Vuoden nuori taiteilija / Årets unga konstnär / Young Artist of the Year

Taidemuseo Meilahti
Tamminiementie 6, 00250 Helsinki
Puh. (09) 310 87031
Avoinna ti–su 11-18.30
Lipar 6/5 €, alle 18-v. ilmaiseksi
Perjantaisin ilmainen sisäänpääsy

www.taidemuseo.fi

Taidemuseo Meilahti

2

1

3

LEVI'S® BLUE POP UP STORE
LAUNCH PARTY
20/03/2008
21H∙00 - 02H∙00

In Collaboration With:
CLINIC
DE BURBURESTRAAT 5
ANTWERPEN - SOUTH

EXCLUSIVE LIVE CONCERT
22H∙00
FANCLUB DJ'S

LEVI'S® BLUE POP UP STORE
OPEN FROM:
21/03-21/05/2008

WWW.LEVIS.BE

4

1-2. Design of the invitation, posters and part of
the installation of the exhibition *Yours Truly*, by the
contemporary artist Heta Kuchka in the Museum
of the City of Helsinki.

3-4. Design of posters, invitations and typography for
a pop-up Levi's store in Antwerp, Belgium. A single ink
was used for all these graphic elements.

Design of several album covers for the record label Eskimo Recordings.

marimekko

Marimekko Thin
Marimekko Light
Marimekko Book
Marimekko Bold
Marimekko Black

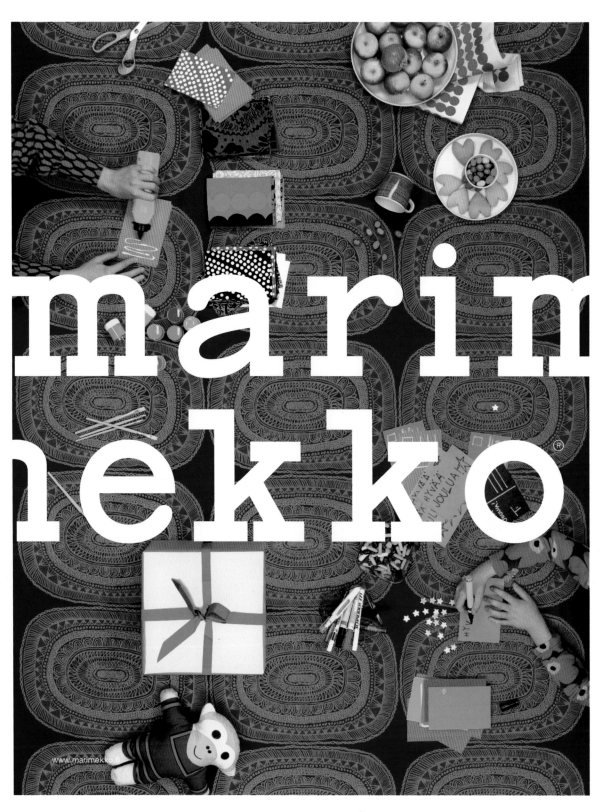

Several works of art direction and design for the textile company Marimekko, of which Chris Bolton has been the art director since 2000. The works include the redesign of the brand's logo and creation of the typeface.

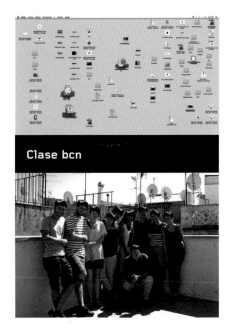

Clase bcn

Barcelona, Spain
www.clasebcn.com

Clase bcn is a graphic design and visual communications studio in Barcelona, founded by Claret Serrahima in 1978. We are a young, international and multidisciplinary team that has received awards on several occasions. We cover all areas of design from corporate identity and branding to packaging, publishing, art direction... with a specific emphasis on typography and the element of surprise as well as a coherent and rigorous handling of the specific needs of each commission. When we take on a project, no matter what size, we take care of each stage of the strategic and creative process, seeking specific, innovative and distinctive approaches, but always focusing on the end objective.

Corporate identity for the restaurant Bravo, by Carlos Abellan, at the Hotel W in Barcelona. The elegant typography and fine materials such as wood, match the concept of the restaurant.

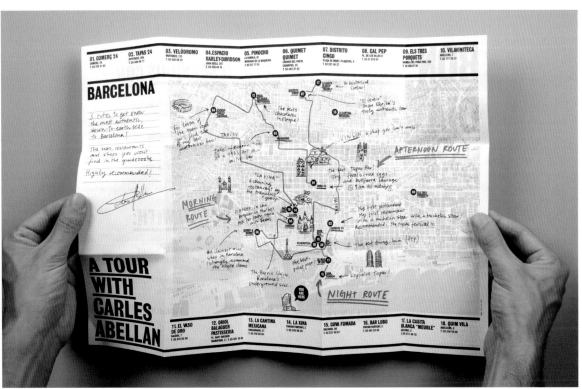

Corporate identity for contemporary Art center Arts Santa Mònica in Barcelona. The logo with the letter A is part of the visual poem that is created in the absence of the letters A in the name of the center.

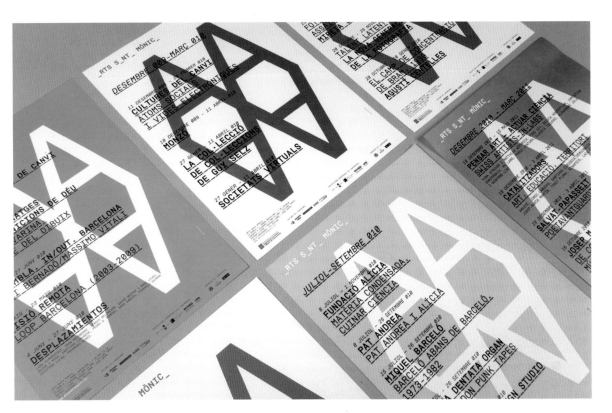

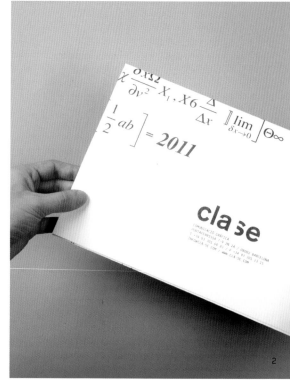

1-2. Christmas card from the studio. It includes a complicated formula to survive 2011.

3. Contemporary design with classic spirit for the label of the quality wines La Fou, by the winery Roqueta Origen.

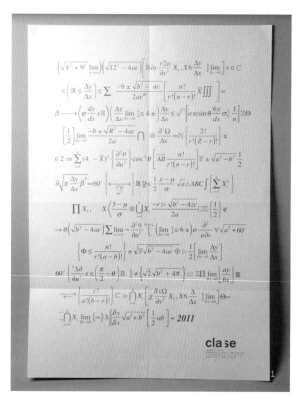

Image for the temporary boutique Sita Murt, open in Sitges in summer only. The identity is based on a handwritten font with fluorescent colors that add a modern look.

Design of the fall winter 2010-2011 catalog for the high-end shoe label Pedro García.

pedro garcía
autumn-winter
2010/2011

COEN!

Eindhoven, the Netherlands
www.coen.info

I'm Coen van Ham (1971), a Dutch conceptual designer, architectural designer and source of creative inspiration. After studying at the Design Academy in Eindhoven, I established my own design agency COEN! It offers innovative concepts, effective and much talked about designs and inspiring identity design management. Everyone is unique. We at COEN! have the expertise and the people needed to translate this uniqueness into a consistent and powerful identity which fits you like a glove.

These new offices are designed to be the headquarters of two organizations dedicated to education. The interior design and corporate identity sought a visual connection between the common objectives of both institutions.

The offices of the Dutch Association of Colleges and Schools for Adults were designed with the aim of creating a bright and attractive work space.

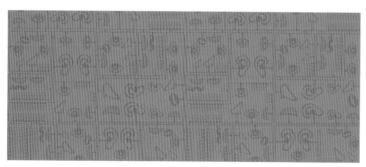

The visual identity of the Friso organization, dedicated, among other activities, to the organization of gay parties and events, represents love with two identical triangles that touch by their vertices, forming a kaleidoscope.

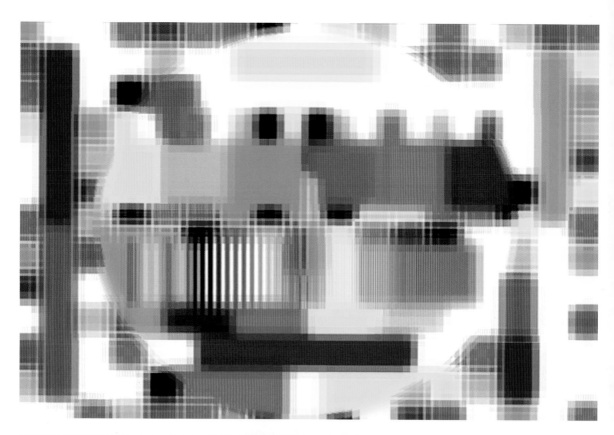

Interior Design of Offices for the National Television Channel, based on the image of a test card.

Personal project inspired by the designer's visit to
Shanghai in 2010 and that relates art, speed and
innovation with nature and tradition.

Côme de Bouchony

Paris, France
www.comedebouchony.com

I am a Paris-based independent designer and art director who has been
running his studio since 2007. Before
that, I studied graphic design at Esag
Penninghen in Paris, France, and
Willem de Kooning Academie in Rotterdam, The Netherlands. The studio works in cultural and commercial
fields and specializes in print design. I
have worked with the likes of *The New
York Times*, *Wad Magazine*, Lacoste,
Condé Nast, Kemistry Gallery, BETC
EuroRSCG, Arte and Domino Records,
among others.

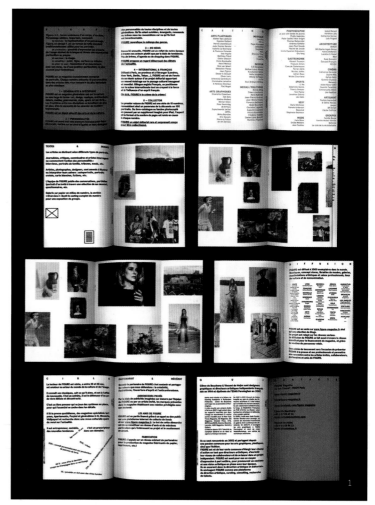

1-2. *Figure Magazine*, designed in collaboration with Vincent de Hoÿm, is a
cultural magazine on the latest trends in art, music, food, architecture, etc.

FIGURE

1
FIGURE is 10 people to admire each issue.
2
FIGURE is an ongoing investigation on art de vivre.
3
FIGURE is not a news magazine.
4
FIGURE is your ideal dinner casting.
5
FIGURE is selective ideas for popular audience.
6
FIGURE is sunshine behind that rain.
7
FIGURE is made with words, pictures and bananas.
8
FIGURE is generalist & specific.
9
FIGURE is celebrated and anonymous people.
10
FIGURE is a sexy solution to the problem.

FIGURE loves you.

www.figure-magazine.fr

JUIN 2011
CONFIDENTIEL

FIGURE PRESS KIT

2

This book-catalog, of which only 250 copies were published, is a compilation of the complete works of Elvire Bonduelle, entitled *Les dessins à la règle. Catalogue raisonné.* Published by Onestar Press in 2011.

Les Bouquineries Oxfam récupèrent des livres en bon état et les revendent à prix réduits pour financer les actions d'Oxfam France. Secousse soutient cette initiative en ouvrant un nouvel espace de lecture, d'information, et de détente sur la mezzanine du Bar du Comptoir Général. Oxfam compte sur vos dons pour enrichir la sélection culturelle proposée, et recherche aussi des bénévoles quelques heures pendant le week-end.

LA BIBLIOTHÈQUE

ÉTÉ samedi 16h – 20h dimanche 12h – 20h	**RENTRÉE** vendredi et samedi 16h – 20h dimanche 12h – 20h

design — Olivye de Bouchony – 2011.

Oxfam
La Bouquinerie

Oxfam France est une association de solidarité internationale qui lutte contre les injustices et la pauvreté dans le monde.

SECOUSSE

Le Bar du Comptoir Général
80 quai de Jemmapes, 75010 Paris, France.

Le Bar du Comptoir Général in Paris is a space that combines a bar, museum and cultural center. The posters advertise various activities carried out here, using the ghetto as a main theme.

FRIDAY 1ST JULY

LONDON

— Petit enfant surnommé Mowgli dans la jungle

SECOUSSE

4

UPROOT ANDY SPECIAL GUEST

- **A.J. HOLMES,** DJS
MOROKA, VAMANOS, K-STRO

NOTTING HILL ARTS CLUB

www.secousse.org
facebook.com/secousseltd

00 12.3

FRIDAY 3RD JUNE

1

— Artist Paa Joe sculpts custom-built wooden coffins in Ghana

SECOUSSE

LONDON

LIVE: **THE HACKNEY EMPIRE**
DJS: **A.J. HOLMES, MOROKA, VAMANOS, K-STRO**

NOTTING HILL ARTS CLUB

www.secousse.org
facebook.com/secousseltd

00 12.3

SAMEDI 4 JUIN   Siestes Électroniques
DANS LES JARDINS DU

Quai Branly

15H - 19H

entrée libre

— Vivianne Sassen - Dust

S E C O U S S E

Paris

2

DJ TRON
(SPECIAL ARABIC REVOLUTION SET)
MO DJ
(SPECIAL MALI SET)
MO LAUDI
(SPECIAL VAUDOO SET)

www.secousse.org
facebook.com/secousseltd

MUSÉE DU (www.) QUAI BRANLY (.fr)
37, QUAI BRANLY
75007 → PARIS.

SECOUSSE Pré**sente**

SHANGAAN ELECTRO

à point éphémère

24 JUIN

POINT ÉPHÉMÈRE

nova

BRAIN

TSUGI

PARIS

— Tshetsha Boys

N O Z I N J A
(AFRIQUE DU SUD) **Tiyiselani Vomaseve**
Nkata Mawewe
and the tshetsha boys

F E A D Z (FRANCE)

Mo Laudi (AFRIQUE DU SUD)

SECOUSSE

3

www.secousse.org
www.pointephemere.org

00H / 6H | 14 / 16 EUROS
POINT ÉPHÉMÈRE—
200 QUAI DE VALMY | 75010 PARIS.

The Secousse is an art space focused on the exotic and unusual world of the ghetto. The posters illustrate different events carried out in this space.

Brochure-guide on the activities of La Secousse. Three ink print on recycled paper.

This series of posters researches the relationship between music and typography in three pieces of work that pay tribute to the music of Metronomy, Larytta and Serge Gainsbourg.

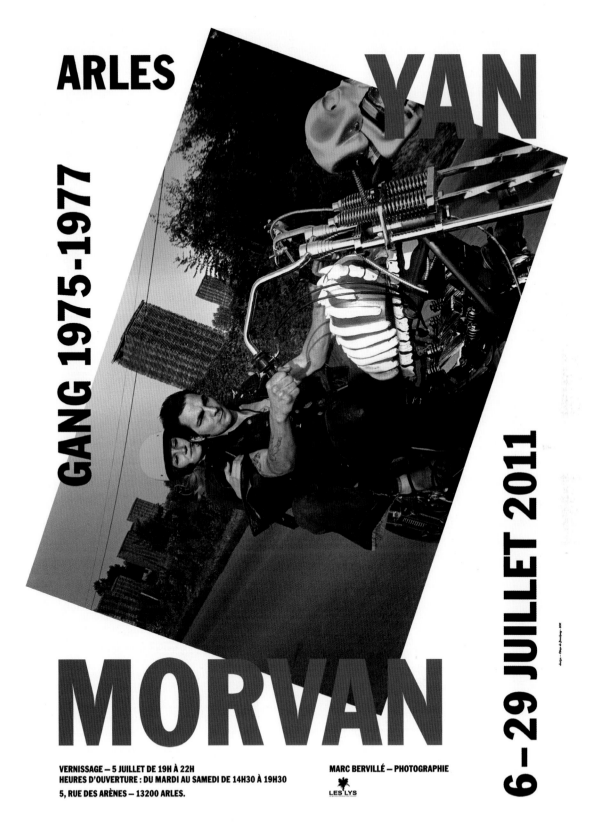

ARLES

GANG 1975-1977

YAN

MORVAN

6 – 29 JUILLET 2011

VERNISSAGE – 5 JUILLET DE 19H À 22H
HEURES D'OUVERTURE : DU MARDI AU SAMEDI DE 14H30 À 19H30
5, RUE DES ARÈNES – 13200 ARLES.

MARC BERVILLÉ – PHOTOGRAPHIE
LES LYS

Invitation to the photography exhibition *Yan Morvan-Gang 1975-1977* in the Photography Festival from Arles. Silver-plated, violet and black ink on glossy paper.

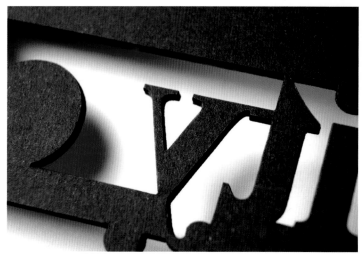

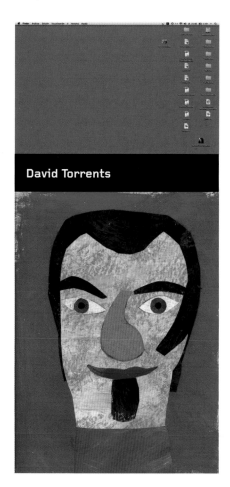

David Torrents

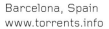

Barcelona, Spain
www.torrents.info

I am a multidisciplinary graphic designer based in Barcelona. I love to design posters, websites, books, graphic identities, environmental designs and motion. I have a degree from Gerrit Rietveld Academie in Amsterdam and from the Faculty of Fine Arts at the University of Barcelona, I also studied at Elisava School for Design in Barcelona. Prior to creating my own studio I worked in Amsterdam, Budapest, and in various studios and agencies in Barcelona. I published and I exhibited my work in several cities around the world.

Catalogue for an exhibition at the Museum of Decorative Arts in Barcelona in which it reflects the importance of emptiness and the negative on industrial design.

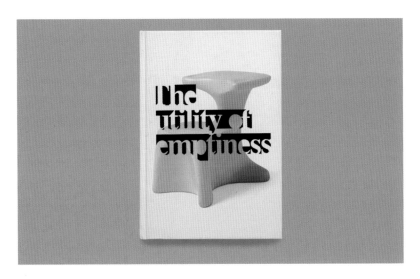

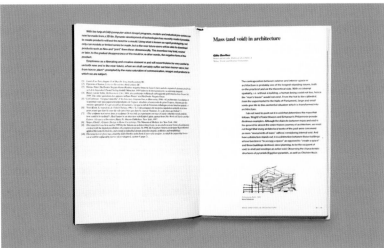

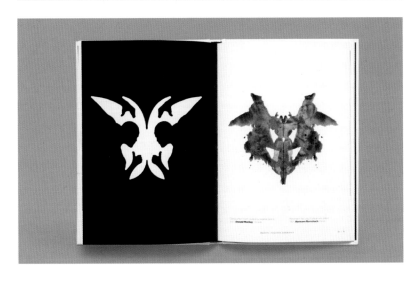

20km/h

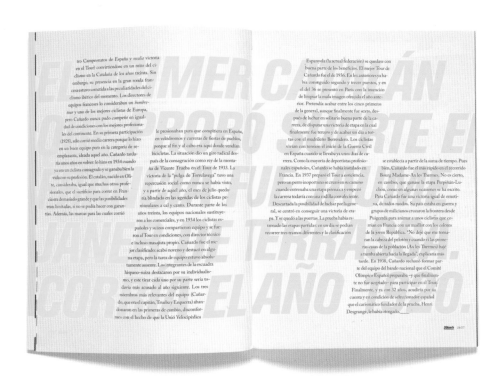

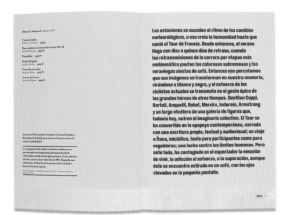

Design of the specialist urban bike magazine *20 km/h*, for the client Bike Tech.

One of the posters of a series designed for El Grec, a Barcelona Summer festival of theater, music and dance.

Design of a poster from the interaction of the shapes of the letters that make up the logo CoNCA (Consell de la Cultura i les Arts).

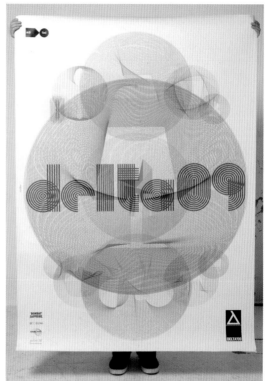

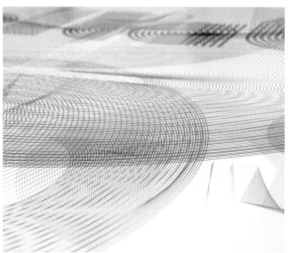

Various designs for the Delta awards, industrial design awards given by the FAD (Foment de les Arts Decoratives).

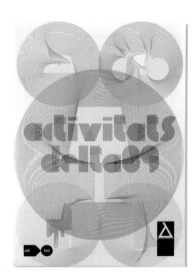

Editorial design of *El que es menjava a casa*, book edited
by Riurau and that compiles the culinary experience of
three generations of a family from Gerona, Spain.

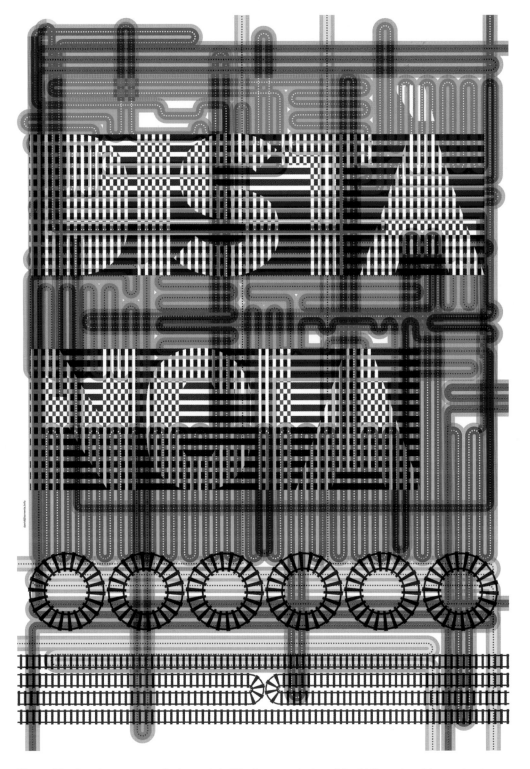

The multinational paper manufacturer Arjo Wiggins commissioned David Torrents with a poster to promote its collection of papers.

Deanne Cheuk
(Hugo & Marie)

New York, NY, USA
www.deannecheuk.com

Deanne Cheuk is a New York-based
art director, illustrator and artist. She
has been commissioned by companies
such as American Express, Levi's,
Nike, Converse, Swatch, Target, MTV,
Nickelodeon, The Gap, Urban Outfitters, *The Guardian*, *T Magazine* and
The New York Times Magazine for her
illustrative and stylistic approach.
Cheuk's artwork is inspired by nature, utopia, space and being, often
distorting realistic representation
into fantasy. Her first book is called
Mushroom Girls Virus.

Illustration in B/W created on behalf of the magazine *American Rag Magazine*.

Photo Illo is the name of a series of illustrations carried out by the photographer Coliena Rentmeester.

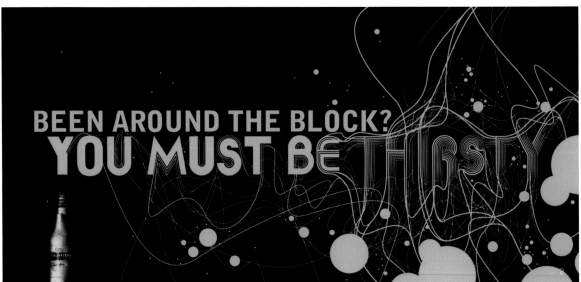

1. *April* illustration for the magazine *Fast Company*.

2. An advertising campaign for Miller Genuine Draft.

White Light, illustration created for AIGA New York, the Professional Association for Design.

TOKION

THE SOUND OF NOW

GOES

With

Lou Reed

Yoko Ono

Nick Cave

Mike Kelley

Cat Power

plus

Phishheads,

Furries

and Sudanese

Fundamentalists

$4.95US $6.95CAN

Art direction and design of the typeface for the magazine *Tokioni*, between 2002 and 2005.

Dennis Koot

The Hague, the Netherlands
http://koot.nu

My name is Dennis Koot, born in 1976 in a village named Limmen, in the north-west of Holland. I studied at the Royal Academy in The Hague some years ago and I'm still living there. After graduating, I worked for five years at the Studio Dumbar and since 2006 I have been self employed. My interests include fashion, British music, laughing, doing sports (lately) and going out till late. I like to keep my work as diverse as the things I am interested in. I guess that's why I became a graphic designer; it covers many other aspects of the art and design disciplines. In each project I try to work with other people as much as possible. If not, this job can be very lonely...

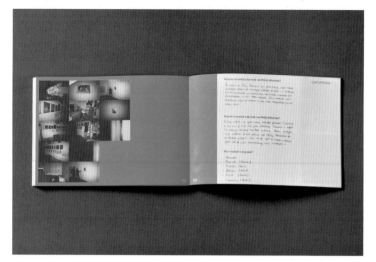

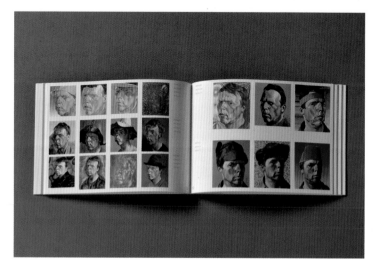

The exhibition catalog by Philip Akkerman incorporates the idea of a sticker album, which are included with the book. In this way, you can emulate collectors and complete the collection of the artists' portraits.

The posters announce several collective exhibitions, by artists and students of art and design academies.

1.Wall painting for the exhibition by the artist Philip Akkerman in the art gallery Torch.

2-3. Stationery design for the information services company Joep Schrijft, belonging to the journalist Joep van Zijl. The typography is reminiscent of that of the newspapers for which he works.

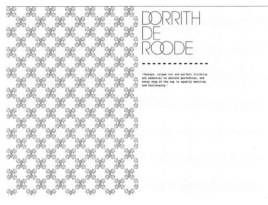

Design of the corporate image and of the web of the fashion designer Dorrith de Roode. The visitor's card is also a small catalog printed on thin paper.

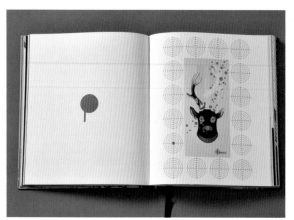

The book *Contemporary Embroidery* offers a unique insight into the work and the creative processes of the artist Ton of Holland.

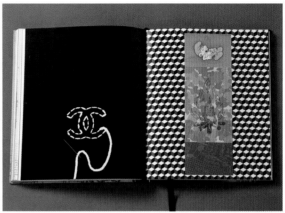

Death never sleeps

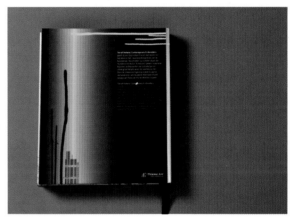

This volume, designed in collaboration with the artist Ton Hoogerwerf, showcases the sketches, details, sources of inspiration and reserves of the painter's works.

Eight Branding Design

Tokyo, Japan
www.8brandingdesign.com

I was born in 1976 in Shiga, Japan, and I am a branding designer currently working as a CEO of Eight Branding Design. I have previously worked for the development of various corporate brands, products, and shops using a wide genre of designs such as graphic, product, and interior. My major works include the brand designs for the premium craft beer Coedo, green tea café Nana's Green Tea, Kintetsu Corporation Uehommachi Yufura, and Kirin beverage Namacha. In the meantime, I have also received various honorable awards and published several books.

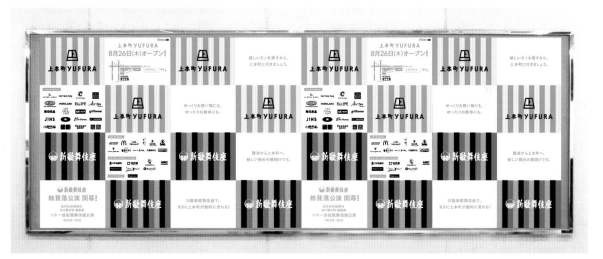

Image for the Uehommachi Yufura complex, in Osaka, a building with shops and offices. The corporate image was used in the building and elsewhere in the city, like the subway.

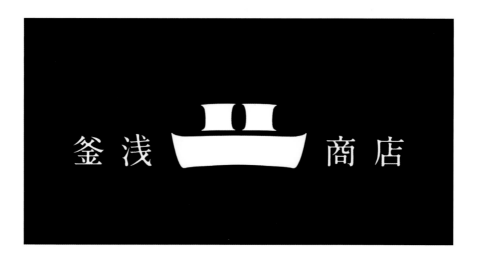

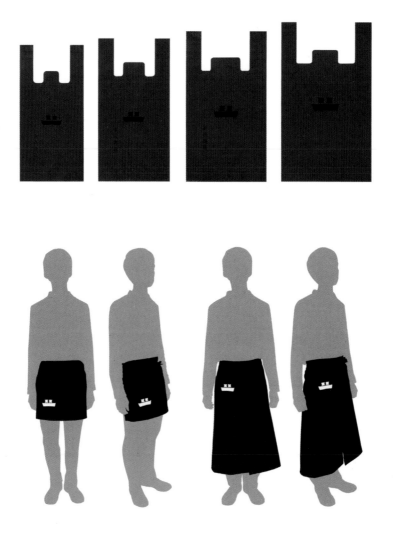

Corporate image for a kitchenware store which celebrates its centenary anniversary. Black is used as a base color and the logo is applied to packaging, wrapping paper, stationery, web, etc.

白庭台幼稚園

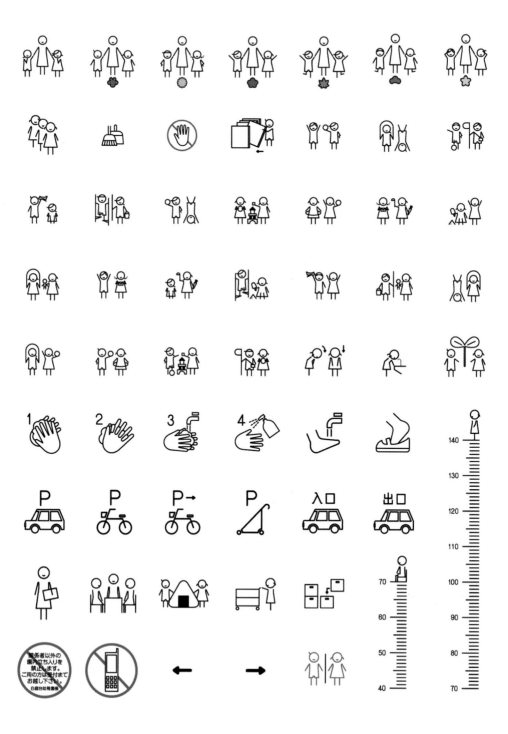

Pictograms for the Shironiwadai kindergarten school.
The pictograms indicate spaces and actions.

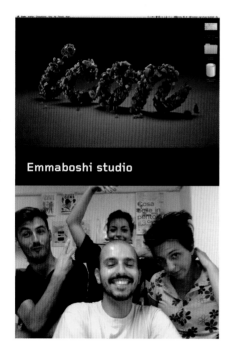

Emmaboshi studio

Bologna, Italy
www.emmaboshi.net

Emmaboshi is a graphic and web design studio based in Bologna, Italy, formed by Emanuele Centola, Martina Galetti, Andrea De Carolis and Erica Scigliuolo. The studio designs for both print solutions and the web, using simplicity to keep things just that, simple, so that everyone can understand them. On the web the studio uses HTML5 and CCS3. The studio wants to be very proud of the projects and that's why it works with great dedication and commitment. Emmaboshi studio likes to observe, listen and suggest; to be curious, young and creative.

Design of a commemorative box for the 40th anniversary of the Autonomous Region of Emilia-Romagna. The box includes a picture book, a copy of the status of the region and a double DVD.

Design of the image and graphic elements for the traveling movie festival Libero Cinema in Libera Terra. It includes poster, shirt, bag and postcards.

Art direction for Lista Civica election campaign during Bologna's municipal elections in 2011. The logo, posters, bags, postcards and programs were designed.

Design of the DVD and the 32-page booklet accompanying it, of the documentary *My Main Man*, which is about jazz in Bologna, produced by Bottega Bologna and Articolture and directed by Germano Maccioni.

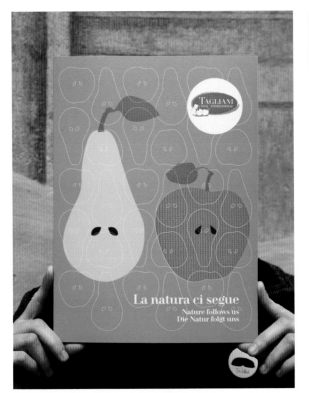

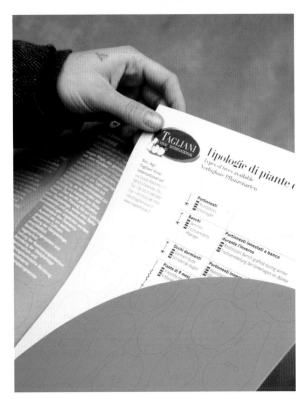

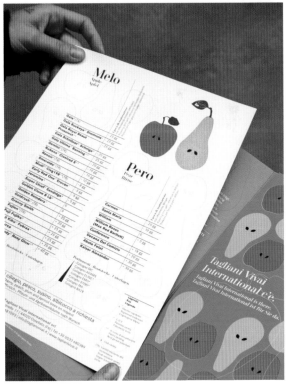

Design of a promotional brochure and corporate folder for Tagliani Vivai International, a company that trades with high quality fruit. The illustrations are inspired by the work of Iela Mari.

The studio Emmaboshi was commissioned by Zizi Collective with the catalog design, poster and invitation for the exhibition *Superheroes on the Sofa*.

In the exposition which took place in the Bologna's Children's Book Fair in 2010,
14 unpublished illustrations of favorite superheroes by 14 illustrators were presented.

EstudioFbdi®

Buenos Aires, Argentina
www.estudiofbdi.com

Fbdi is a creative studio with offices in the city of Buenos Aires. Our goal is to provide each project with ideas to express and unfold the potential of the brands. We believe in the impact of design and ideas and apply these concepts to branding and brand communication. Federico Batemarco, director of the studio, founded Fbdi over 10 years ago with the intention of creating and enhancing local and international brands through graphic and industrial design and art direction. With a strong experience in luxury brands and fashion brands, the studio works in different industries and segments.

Cresud is the leading Argentinean company in the agricultural sector. On the occasion of its 75th anniversary, a book was designed that covers all work carried out in the company through text and images.

Frank's is a speakeasy bar in Buenos Aires, a secret bar inspired by locals from New York at the time of Prohibition. The brand image and graphics of the premises were inspired by materials and textures that refer to the 20's.

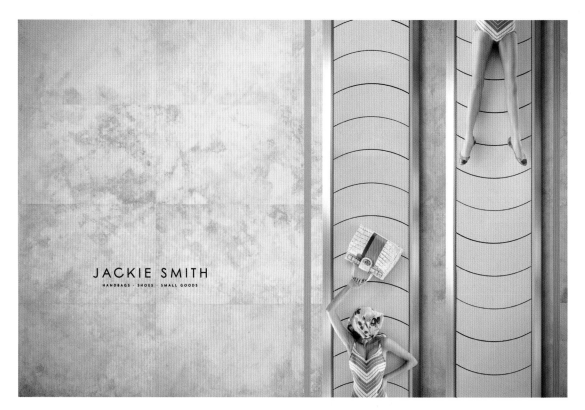

Identity for the handbag and shoe company Jackie Smith. From the brand name and the slogan of affordable luxury, an identity was defined that reflects a feminine, classical, international, romantic, timeless and sophisticated world.

The design for the company Odille, a very famous multi-brand store in Buenos Aires, is feminine, romantic, and with a personality that is expressed in contrasts, superimpositions and diversity of textures.

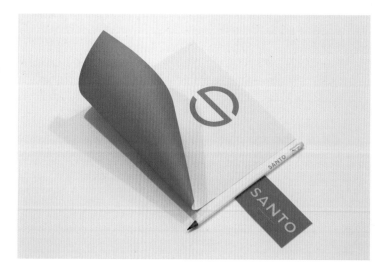

Redesign of the identity of the Santo advertising agency. A rationalist aesthetic with clean, simple lines that highlight the essential was used.

Design of the Patio Bullrich mall campaign in Buenos Aires, in which the theme is the diversity of ways of looking. The artist Edgardo Gimenez uses vision-related objects to create images.

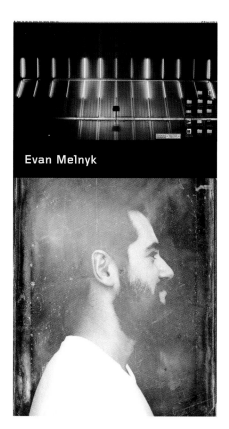

Evan Melnyk

Montreal, Canada
www.curseofthemultiples.com

BIG BIGGER. BETTER. These three words describe the graphic designer, artist and a compulsive consumer of carbonated beverages Evan Melnyk. His favorite movies are the same as yours. Evan Melnyk enjoys playing music and daydreaming. And most importantly, he moonlights as a body double for Prince (when not busy painting or designing products, magazines, websites, or clothing). Some of his clients include 2K by Gingham, Spitfire Sunglasses, Furni Creations, Holiday Matinee and Bongo Beat Records. His work has appeared in books such as *The Big Book of Bags, Tags, and Labels* and *Best of Poster Design*.

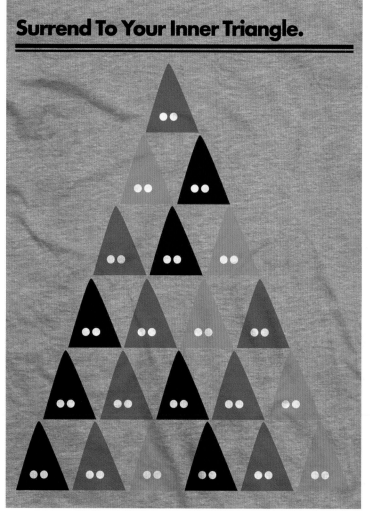

T-shirts designs for Asian label Graniph, online clothing store.

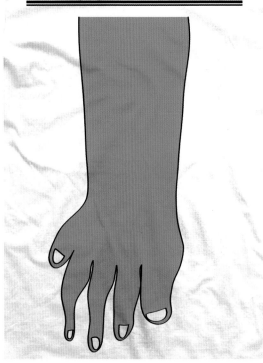

HEAD IN THE CLOUDS

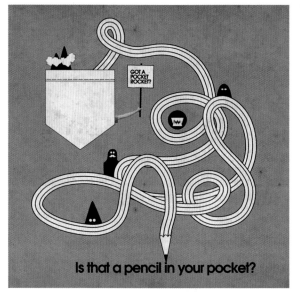

Various illustrations for fanzines. They also serve as an endorsement for the designer.

Illustrations for *New Sugar Magazine*, digital version of printed publication.

THE
FUTURE
LOOKS
BRIGHT.

BRIGHTER WORLD
Who'd have thought the grey streets
of London could have spawned
something so bright. Introducing
the Spitfire Winter 2011 Collection.
A range of sunglasses, including
our new Premium Acetate Line, and
headphones that make every day
just a little bit brighter.

Catalog for winter 2011 collection of the sunglass label Spitfire.

Juste un garçon.

Juste une fille.

Two designs for T-shirts by the Japanese label 2K by Gingham.

Feed

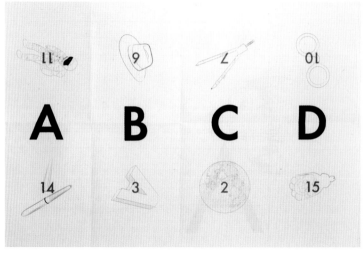

Montreal, Canada
www.studiofeed.ca

We at Feed eat a bit of anything printed, as well as some of what's on screen or in space. We are an independent graphic design studio based in Montreal, specializing in branding, publishing and typeface design. But we work in many formats, be it print, exhibition, event or spatial design, websites or motion graphics. The studio's work, benefiting from a straight-forward approach, has garnered numerous awards, been the subject of conferences and exhibits, and has been published both in Quebec and abroad.

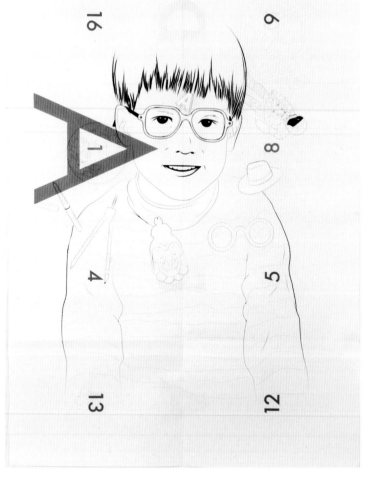

The project *A1* consists of a poster and a brochure for the Media Lab at Concordia University in which the career aspirations of a young Daniel Canty are narrated starting with the letter A. Illustrations by Stéphane Poirier.

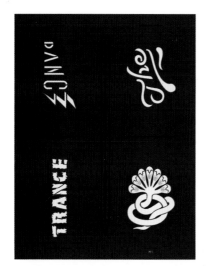

The project *Crayon Noir no. 1* is part of the blog *Crayon Noir* (http://crayonnoir.tumblr.com), in which images and words are associated.

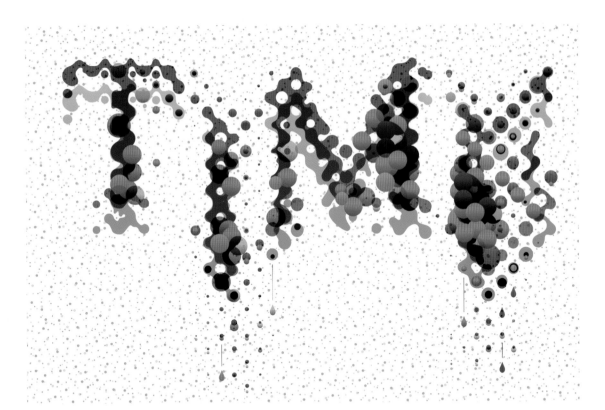

Illustration with the theme of transformation for the second issue of the journal *Pica*.

Pliage n°01

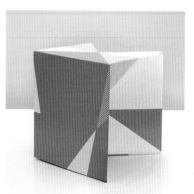
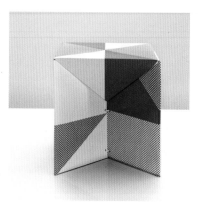
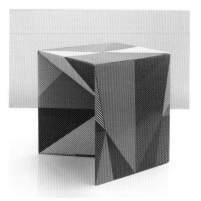

The screenprinted cardboard stool *Ottopapax* was created for a group exhibition. Photography by Simon Duhamel.

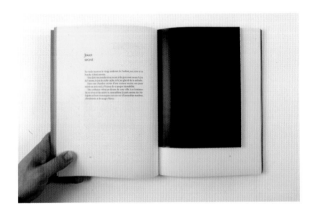

Poetic anthology *Le Livre de chevet*, edited by Daniel Canty. The margins and the paper color change throughout the book as a symbol of the course of sleep. The illustrations are by Annie Descoteaux and Pol Turgeon.

Folch Studio

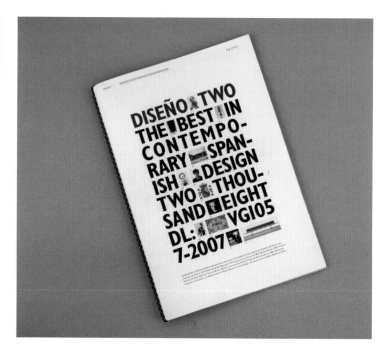

Barcelona, Spain
http://folchstudio.com

Folch Studio was born in 2004 in the city of Barcelona, directed and managed by me. The studio specializes in editorial design, art direction, publicity, corporative image, website and video. We work with national and international clients such as Marset, Mishima, *Tiger Magazine*, Desigual, Sirex, Fundació Miró, Mango, *Metal*, Silver, Pull&Bear, MUSAC, Generalitat de Catalunya, Furest, MARCO, Trucco, Tiger, Friday's Project, Beefeater, ICUB, Fanzine137, FAD, Camper, Marset, Florentino, Joan Morey, TV3/C33... The studio's work has been selected and nominated for several LAUS awards from 2005 until the present day and in 2008 the studio received two LAUS awards. The studio's work has also been selected for the *Daniel Gil Awards* 2005, 2006, 2007, 2008, and received an award in 2007. Furthermore, the studio received silver in the *Design Week Awards* in London 2008.

Design Magazine, made for Origin Communications, by the Spanish Foreign Trade Institute (ICEX).

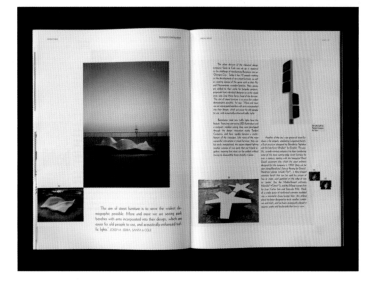

Art direction, packaging, corporate identity and advertising for the
multi-brand clothing store Furest.

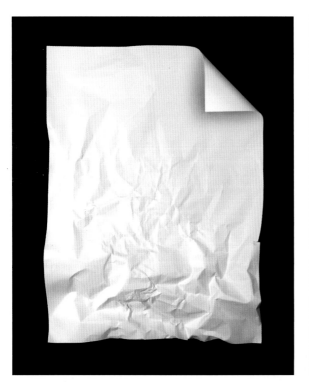

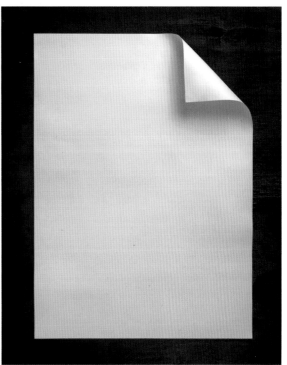

Posters from the series *Icons*, a collection of various projects and personal works.

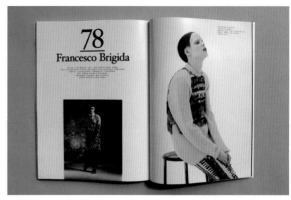

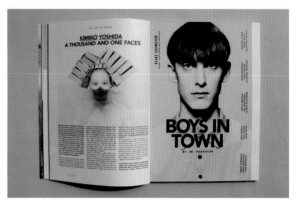

Design and art direction for fashion and trends magazine *Metal*.

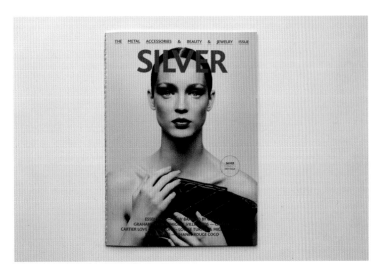

Design of the first issue of *Silver*, a journal published by the magazine *Metal*.

Design and art direction of the magazine *Tiger*, a biannual publication on contemporary creativity.

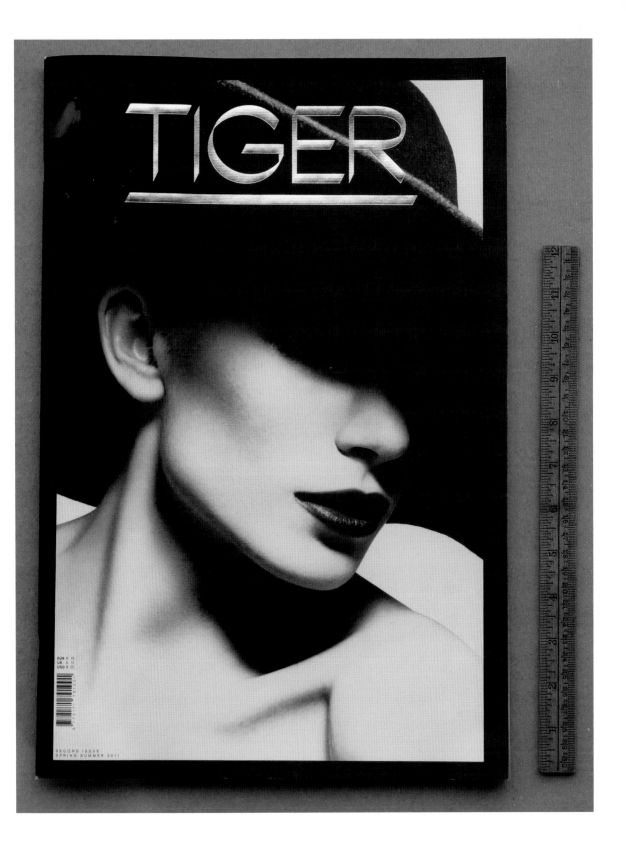

Foreign Policy Design

Singapore, Singapore
www.foreignpolicydesign.com
www.yahlengyu.com

I am a creative director + art director
+ designer + idea maker + story teller
+ problem solver all in one. I do everything to bring a design to fruition.
I attended the Art Institute of Boston
before moving to New York City where
I was lucky enough to work with some
of the most interesting names in the
world including Versace, Bvlgari, Vi-
vienne Westwood, Oscar de la Renta,
Ferragamo, Sisley etc. I am currently
based in Singapore where I founded
Foreign Policy Design Group.

Promotional project to welcome your arrival to Singapore from New York by the agency Yah-Leng Yu. It consists of a calendar, business card and label.

Corporate image for the French restaurant Cocotte located in the Indian district of Singapore. The old aesthetics of French eateries was used.

Corporate image of the hotel The Waterhouse. An attractive and international image has been sought, operating in both Shanghai and Berlin. The duality between modernity and tradition of the city, white and black, etc is played with.

1. Packaging Design for *Second Skin* Innolab, a clear and lightweight cover for iPhone mobiles. The design contrasts a heavy industrial aesthetic with the lightness of the product.

2. Redesign of business cards of a music laboratory. The design can be stamped with inkpads on recycled paper, meaning they do not have to be printed and help towards sustainability.

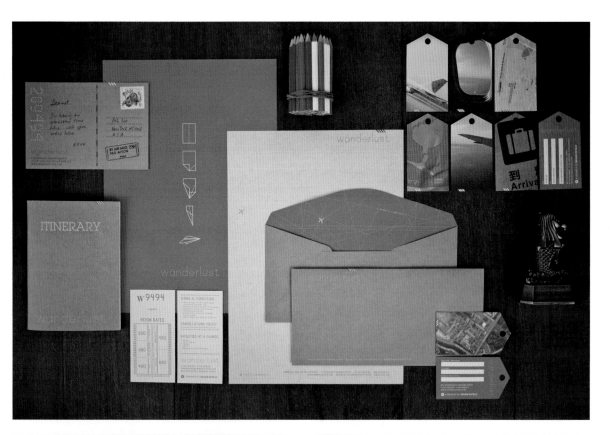

Corporate image of Wanderlust hotel in Singapore.
The design evokes the meaning of the word *wanderlust*:
desire to travel. Everything has to do with travel
memorabilia: travel tickets, museums tickets etc.

George Tsioutsias

London, UK
http://tearapart.tv

Greek-born Londoner George Tsiout-sias' career took off at the tender age of nine, when he received a pan-European award in painting. After receiving a first in communication design from the Chelsea College of Arts & Design, George spent years designing and art directing for branding, music and fashion. His creative interests converged on the medium of moving image, and flew him right across the Atlantic where he landed at Interspectacular New York. Upon returning to London he set up Tearapart.tv with fellow artist Theo Michael. Tearapart.tv quickly amassed broad recognition and a reputable reel of idents, shorts and promos, boasting work for David LaChapelle and an onedotzero award-winning video for Ebony Bones. George's multidisciplinary background allows him to work across a wide range of formats including music & fashion videos, commercials, title sequences, virals and branded content.

Frames for *Black Widow*, Coco Electrik music video, electropop band formed by singer-songwriter Anne Booty and producer Paul Harrison.

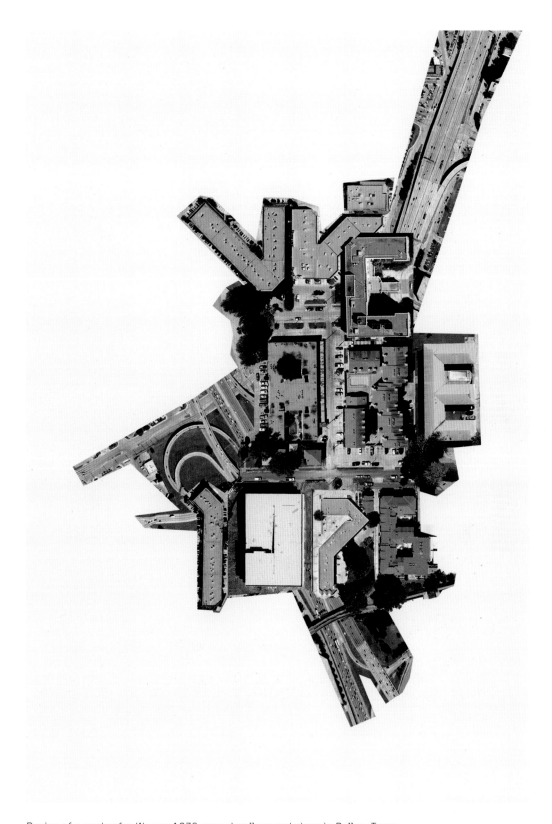

Design of a poster for We are 1976, an art gallery and store in Dallas, Texas.

Poster with monthly programming for the Ditched Disco nightclub. The aesthetic is similar to that of noticeboards.

Promotional images for the Ditched Disco nightclub in Shoreditch, London.

Frames from the videoclip *Fire & Ice* by the band Coco
Electrik.

1. Promotional illustration by the designer for the website of his company Tearapart.tv.

2. TEAR, the alter ego of the designer George Tsioutsias and his partner Theo Michael, is the designer of album covers for the Berlin discography These Days.

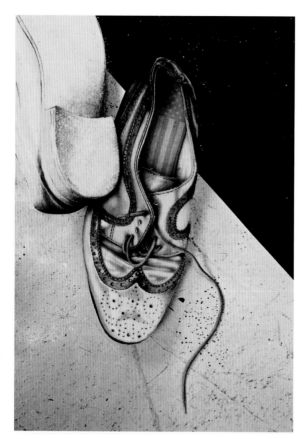

Illustrations for the magazine *Susology*. One of them is
a portrait of the musician Damon Albarn (Blur, Gorillaz)
and another was carried out to illustrate an article about
the Beat generation.

Hampus Jageland

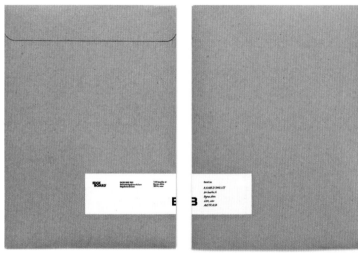

Paris, France
www.hampusjageland.com

I'm a graphic designer, art-director and creative thinker. My approach is inquisitive and collaborative and I believe in big ideas, research and crafted aesthetic. With just two years in the industry, my experience includes work at Saatchi & Saatchi in Sweden, Blue Marlin BD in both Sydney and London, The Creative Method and Maud in Sydney. I graduated from Billy Blue College of Design (Sydney) in 2010 with Honors. As a designer at award winning Sydney-based design studio Maud, I was exposed to all stages of the design process. Clients I worked with include super brands Fosters Group and Toyota to major advertising agencies Publicis Mojo and Whybin TBWA. I am very passionate about design. I undertake each project with a curios and open mind to create meaningful, considered and original images, relevant to the audience as well as the studio and myself.

Corporate image for the kitchen table manufacturer Edgeboard. The edge of the table, the differential component of the wood, is what has been used as the main element of the logo.

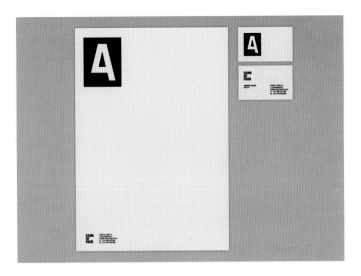

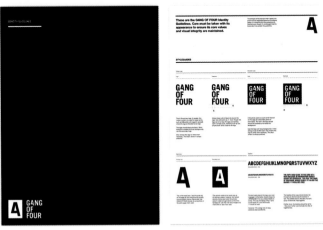

Corporate image for Gang of Four. A modern and clear image was sought that reflected the spirit of the company, dedicated to fusing brands with music.

POSTAGE PAID AUSTRALIA

09 DECEMBER

We're Expanding
An exhibition about big ideas,
expanding out of existing spaces
& exploring new grounds.

You are invited to celebrate
the biggest graduate exhibition
in Billy Blue history.

Gradua
Tuesda
6.00pm
7.30pm

Billy Bl
Mezzan
100 Mi
North S

Open u
10am–

Billy Blue College of Design asked several designers to design the 2009 graduate exhibition. This project highlights the growing number of students and the gradual loss of space.

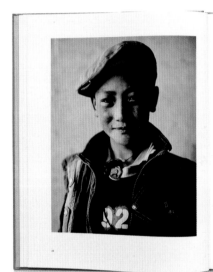

Design of the photography
book on Khampa, Tibet, by the
photographer Tim Roodenrys.
The design moves away from
the typical books on Tibet
and the photography takes the
center stage.

SOHI is a lifestyle magazine, art, culture and fashion of NSW Southern Highlands.

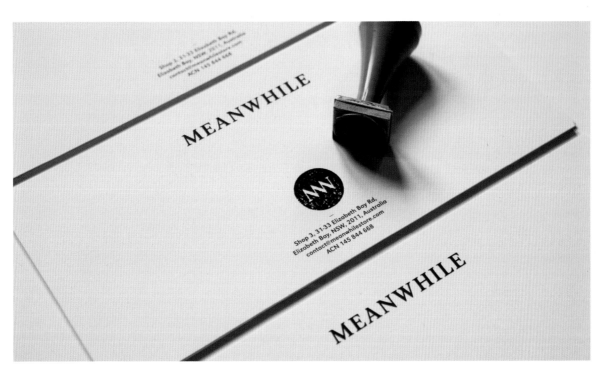

Image for a clothing store with quality labels such as Whyred, Three Over One and Acne. Inkpads were used to give a sense of continuity and customization.

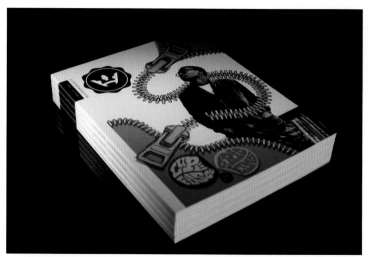

Hatch Berlin

Berlin, Germany
www.hatch-berlin.com

Nina Emmerich and Jens Adamaszek
are founders and managing directors
of Hatch Berlin. Since 2005, we create design concepts together and form
worlds of design for clients from the
fields of art, culture and commerce.
Nina Emmerich: I finished communication design studies at the Potsdam
Technical College and at the Academia
di Belle Arti in Florence. I was already
working as a freelance designer in
Berlin before graduating with a degree
in design with a concentration in moving image and typography.
Jens Adamaszek: I studied at the
Design Akademie Berlin, the Potsdam
Technical College and at the Escolha
Desenha Industrial in Rio de Janeiro,
Brasil. I graduated as a designer with
a concentration in typography and
corporate design.

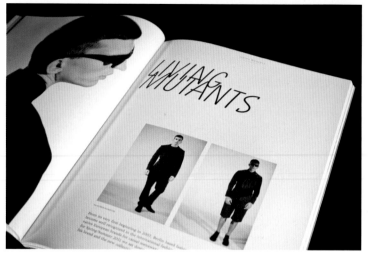

Berlin Hatch designed the layout of *Highsnobiety*, a high profile magazine
about fashion streetwear, sneakers and street art, among other topics.

POINTER X COMME DES GARÇONS

CLARKS X CONCEPTS

COAST TO COAST   KIX 2011 SPRING/SUMMER

This project includes the book design, packaging and image of a line of Villeroy & Boch products.

Corporate image and stationery for the landscaping architecture studio Atelier Loidl.

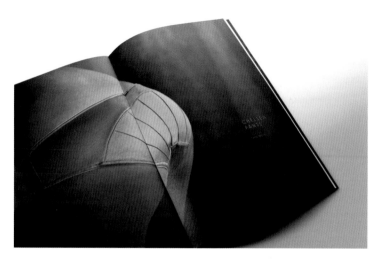

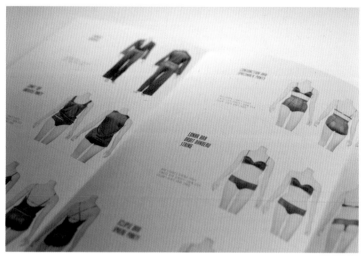

Hatch Berlin is responsible for the design of the web and seasonal catalogs of Wundervoll, a prestigious and exclusive lingerie label based in Berlin.

Jean-Claude Chianale

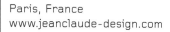

Paris, France
www.jeanclaude-design.com

I am a graphic designer. I was born in France and work and live in Paris. I am a graduate of the École Nationale Superieure des Arts Decoratifs in Paris, and work on different projects in relation with graphic composition, typography and culinary composition. Each project is subject to meticulous research and advanced preparatory studies. I work with artists, architects, designers and choreographers and I have a particular interest in the culinary worlds that I develop through exhibitions in the form of culinary installations.

Design of four postcards for the exhibition *Projects de Villes 2011*. Photography by Julien Magre.

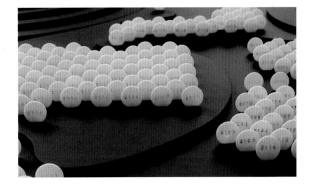

Projects de Villes 2011 is an exhibition that was shown at Galerie Épisodique de París. The work of Jean-Claude Chianale includes a poster, several postcards and an installation of 1000 hosts printed with edible ink.

EN SEPTEMBRE
À L'OCCASION DES JOURNÉES
DU PATRIMOINE,
LE MUSÉE D'ART ET D'HISTOIRE
ET LE PÔLE GRAPHISME
INVITENT
JEAN-CLAUDE CHIANALE.

LA PEINTURE
COMME ACTE SENSUEL,
UNE CRÉATION AU MUSÉE
D'ART ET D'HISTOIRE
TOUS LES JOURS, SAUF LE MARDI, DE 14H À 18H, ENTRÉE : 2€

VOCABULAIRE GRAPHIQUE
PRÉSENTATION DE TRAVAUX
AUX SILOS, MAISON DU LIVRE
ET DE L'AFFICHE
MARDI, JEUDI, VENDREDI 14H-19H, MERCREDI S
FERMÉS LE DIMANCHE ET LE LUNDI GRATUIT

ville de Chaumont

For Heritage Days at the Museum
of Art and History of Chaumont,
Jean-Claude Chianale rediscovers
the works with some posters
showing some of the paintings
and combines them with graphic
elements that emphasize their
sensuality.

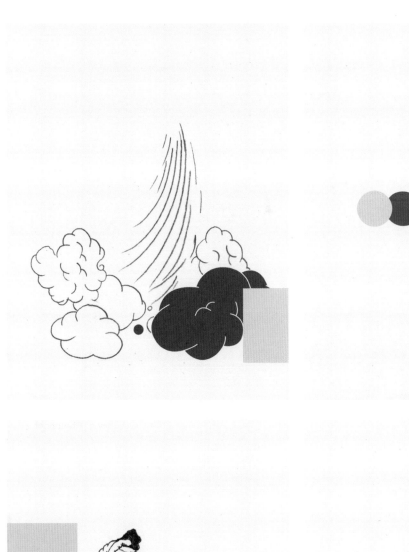

Ironie
Éditions du Sandre
La Galerie épisodique
le 17 juin 2011

de 18h à 7h
entrée libre

Jacques Frézal présente
Le Festival *Ironie* à
LA GALERIE ÉPISODIQUE

La Galerie épisodique
23, passage de Ménimontant
75011 Paris
Métro : Rue St-Maur ou Ménilmontant

T : 01 43 55 03 49
@ : galerieepisodique@prepart.fr

Ironie
LA GALERIE
ÉPISODIQUE

Éditions du Sandre

Librairie du Sandre
5, rue du Marché-Ordener
75018 Paris

*Ironise, a[...]
m'exciter [...]ise
va ! Jean Genet
heureux u[...]
tant, cet instant
c'est ta vie Omar Khayyam
/ Redouter l'iro-
nie, c'est craindre
la raison Sacha Guitry /*

Le Festival *Ironie*
Programmation :
Lionel Dax – Ironie [http://ironie.free.fr]
Jacques Frézal – La Galerie épisodique
Guillaume Zorgbibe – Éditions du Sandre
[www.editionsdusandre.com]

Graphisme, scénographie :
Jean-Claude Chianale [jeanclaude-design.com]
assisté de Sidonie Tarancón-Aymard

Photographie © *Julien Magre* [julien-magre.com]
Projets de villes, Julien Magre et Jean-Claude Chianale

© 2011 *Ironie* / Éditions du Sandre /
Jean-Claude Chianale / La Galerie épisodique.

20h15-6h30 Atelier 1
Paradis / Philippe Sollers
Diffusion de l'enregistrement de *Paradis*
(Seuil, 1981)

*Paradis a toujours été écrit pour être dit.
Ce qui veut dire qu'au moment même où
je l'écrivais, je le vivais, je n'arrêtais pas de le
psalmodier, de le chantonner, de le chuchoter.
Je continue. L'enregistrement effectué par Michel
Gheude et Philippe Berling les 11, 12, 13, 14 et 15
mars 1980, à Paris, est donc la réalisation concrète
de mon intention la plus profonde. Il s'agit pour
moi de laisser se développer et s'épanouir, dans
toutes leurs dimensions, les coïncidences entre le
tracé et la voix, le geste et l'innovation à l'intérieur
même des phrases. Le projet est de raconter le
point où en est arrivée l'espèce humaine.
C'est le roman moderne dans la mesure où
celui qui vit les aventures d'aujourd'hui est
« en direct » avec tout, sans cesse.
Vous écoutez ici le volume 1 de Paradis,
L'ensemble devrait tenir en trois volumes.
Si j'en ai la force et le temps.
Je dédie cet enregistrement à Alban Berg, héros
de la dramaturgie de notre temps.
Je remercie Michel Gheude et Philippe Berling
de leur écoute au moment où la chose s'est faite.
Et, en somme, de leur folie, qui correspond
à la mienne.
À bon entendeur salut.*

Philippe Sollers
[Éditions de Peuguette, 1982]

18h-18h15 Lecture dans le cour
Le Jardinier animiste / Jorn de Précy

18h15-18h35 Atelier 2
La Parole en Deux / Patrice Enard
Projection du film de Patrice Enard,
La Parole en Deux (1974)

18h15-18h40 Atelier 6
Cher Mallarmé / Françoise Dax-
Boyer et Jean-Paul Fargier
Projection de *Cher Mallarmé* (1993), film
de Françoise Dax-Boyer et Jean-Paul Fargier,
avec Judith Magre, Christian Rist et Philippe
Sollers

18h40-19h Atelier 2
Les Demoiselles d'Avignon /
Florence D. Lambert
Projection de la chorégraphie de Florence D.
Lambert, *Les Demoiselles d'Avignon*
(Opéra de Paris, 1993)

18h40-19h Atelier 2
L'art du Maujoin /
Françoise Dax-Boyer
Lecture de *L'art du Maujoin* de Françoise
Dax-Boyer (Ed. de l'Amandier, 2000),
avec Judith Magre et les improvisations
de Laurent Costesèque au saxophone

19h-19h30 Atelier 6
Chantier de la parole /
Marcelin Pleynet
Projection de la parole, texte de Marcelin
Pleynet (*L'Infini* n°83, printemps 2003) :
lecture en public au Centre Georges-
Pompidou le 14 novembre 2002, diffusée
sur « France Culture » le 29 novembre 2002

19h10-19h30 Atelier 2
Radiation & Extraction /
Guy Tournaye et Clément Ribes
Lecture de *Radiation* (Gallimard, 2007)
par l'auteur, Guy Tournaye ; présentation
de la revue et de la collection *Extraction*
par Clément Ribes

19h30-19h40 Atelier 6
Projets de villes / Julien Magre
et Jean-Claude Chianale
Exposition. Inauguration par le futur maire

Panna cotta city, Jean-Claude Chianale
une mise en image de Julien Magre

19h40-20h00 Atelier 2
Rodéo Vidéo / Jean-Paul Fargier
Projection de *Rodéo Vidéo* de Jean-Paul
Fargier, suivie de la présentation du livre,
Ciné et TV vont en vidéo (avis de tempête)
(Ed. De l'Incidence, 2010)

19h40-19h50 Atelier 2
Au tour de Manet / Samuel Rodary
Autour de la publication de *L'art de Manet*
de Jules de Marthold (Ed. de L'Echoppe, 2011),
texte présenté par Samuel Rodary

20h10-22h10 Projection dans la cour
Projection d'un film égyptien
Présentation par Laurent Jeanpierre
et Lionel Dax à 20h

21h-21h20 Atelier 2
Onomabis Repetita /
Compagnie Public Chéri
Onomabis Repetita pièce de Régis Hébette
(2010), pour fêter les 15 ans du Théâtre
de l'Échangeur

21h20-21h30 Atelier 2
Corps-Texte / Lionel Dax
Lecture de *Corps-Texte* (Ed. du Sandre, 2008)
par l'auteur, Lionel Dax

21h30-21h40 Atelier 2
Maximes et Pensées / Nicolas Chamfort
Choix de maximes et de pensées de Chamfort
lues par Léna Bréban et Lionel Dax

21h40-22h Atelier 2
La Bourse ou la Vie / Hervé Rouxel
Lecture de *La Bourse ou la Vie* (*Ironie* n°77,
juillet 2002) par l'auteur, Hervé Rouxel,
et Lionel Dax

22h-22h10 Atelier 2
Le Nouveau site Ironie /
David Guittet
Présentation du nouveau site *Ironie*
par le webmaster d'*Ironie*, David Guittet

22h10-22h20 Atelier 2
**Anti-présentation
de la Librairie du Sandre**
Par Guillaume Zorgbibe et Thomas Feixa
pour fêter l'ouverture de la Librairie
du Sandre, 5 rue du Marché-Ordener,
Paris, XVIII° arrondissement.

22h20-22h30 Atelier 2
Curiosités scientifiques
Choix de films présenté
par les Éditions des Grands champs

22h30-22h50 Atelier 2
Il était temps / Benoît Casas
Lecture de *Il était temps* (Ed. Wharf/Nous,
2010) par l'auteur, Benoît Casas

23h-23h20 Atelier 2
15 ans-15 minutes / Ironie
Projection de *15 ans-15 minutes*,
vidéo réalisée pour les 15 ans d'*Ironie*

23h20-23h40 Atelier 2
Cinéma Expérimental /
Stefani de Loppinot
Projection d'un florilège de films
expérimentaux choisis par Stefani
de Loppinot

Après MINUIT
* Micro-festival Pierre La Police par Crokoos
* *Euphorisme* de Julien Torma
* *Apparadoxus* de Malcolm de Chazal

LIBRAIRIE ÉPHÉMÈRE
Espace de lecture et d'improvisation ouvert
Les Éditions du Sandre, les Éditions
de la Galerie épisodique, les Éditions Nous,
les Éditions Filigrane et autres invités...

23h40-0h00 Atelier 2
Sade actuel /
Joël Person et Frédéric Fontenoy
Lecture par Léna Bréban et Séverine[E]
d'un florilège de textes érotiques, une exposition
de Joël Person et Frédéric Fontenoy

Et deux ou trois surprises...

Poster design and visual identity of the festival Ironie at the Galerie Épisodique.

The design of the exhibition is also run by the designer.
Photos by Julien Magre.

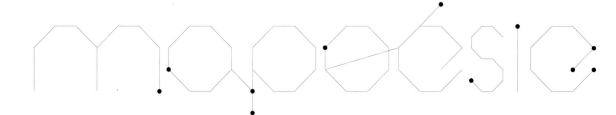

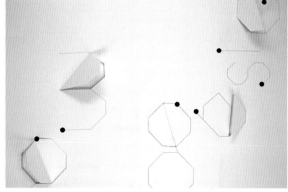

Design of visual identity (including logo, design and production of typography, stationery and website) of Mapoésie, a scarf and fashion accessories label.

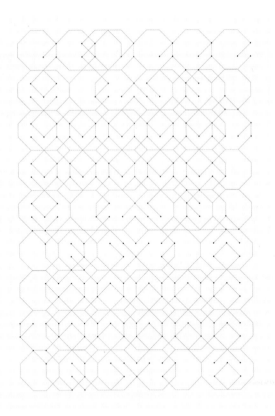

SPRING/SUMMER 2012

MAPOÉSIE
SPRING/SUMMER 2012

SALON 1ÈRE CLASSE – PORTES DE VERSAILLES
HALL 1, STAND K51

3 - 6 SEPTEMBRE 2011

Salon 1ère Classe / 1 Place de la Porte de Versailles – 75015 Paris – France
Mapoésie, Hall 1, stand K51 – *3 to 6 September 2011*

Accès / *Access* :

Métro : ligne 12 - Station *Porte de Versailles*
Bus : Lignes 39 - 49 - PC1 - 80 - *Station Porte de Versailles*
Taxis : Paris expo - Porte de Versailles - hall 1 Porte : L
Tramway : Ligne T2 et T3 - Station *Porte de Versailles*

Horaires d'ouverture / *Opening hours* :

Tous les jours: 9h-19h (mardi : 9h-18h) /
Everyday: 9 am to 7 pm (tuesday : 9 am to 6 pm)

mapoésie

MAPOÉSIE / ELSA POUX SARL • 13, avenue Parmentier - 75011 Paris - France • T.: +33 (0) 6 15 14 58 80
E-mail : elsa.poux@mapoesie.fr • SARL au capital de 15 000 euros • Siren : 523 600 922 • RCS PARIS 523 600 922
TVA intracommunautaire FR07523600922

Photo 2011 © *Mapoésie* / GraphicDesign © j-s-c

www.mapoesie.fr

CCNFC visual identity (Centre Chorégraphique National de Franche-Comté à Belfort / Joanne Leighton). Above: the logo. Bottom left: the programme of activities.

LE JOURNAL DU CCNFCB

Nº 02

JANVIER À JUIN 2011

CENTRE CHORÉGRAPHIQUE NATIONAL DE FRANCHE-COMTÉ À BELFORT

SPECTACLES EN TOURNÉE

CRÉATIONS 2011

Design of the CCNFC magazine and promotion of the dance company's tour.

SPECTACLES EN TOURNÉE

2011-2012

Jules Julien
(Hugo & Marie)

Paris, France
http://julesjulien.com

Jules Julien lives and works in Paris. The work of this artist and illustrator questions the reality of the world around us. He began his career as a personal research project and he has managed to work for important customers such as Diesel, Acer Computer, *Grazia Magazine* and Playstation. He is part of the group Hugo & Marie, a group of artists, designers and illustrators who have come together to promote their work in the U.S.

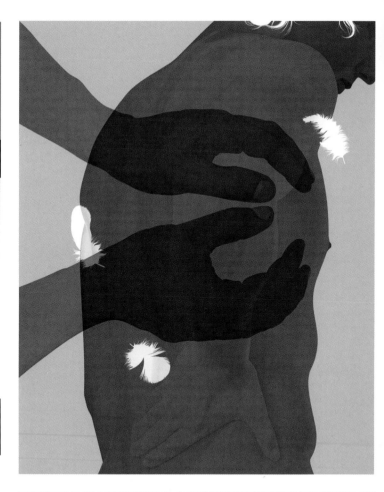

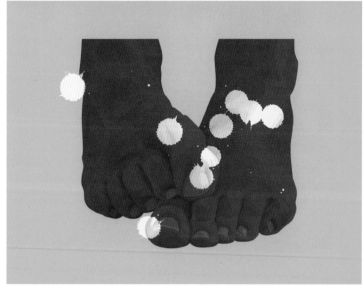

Editorial illustrations for the series *Plaisir* for the French magazine *Têtu*, 2010.

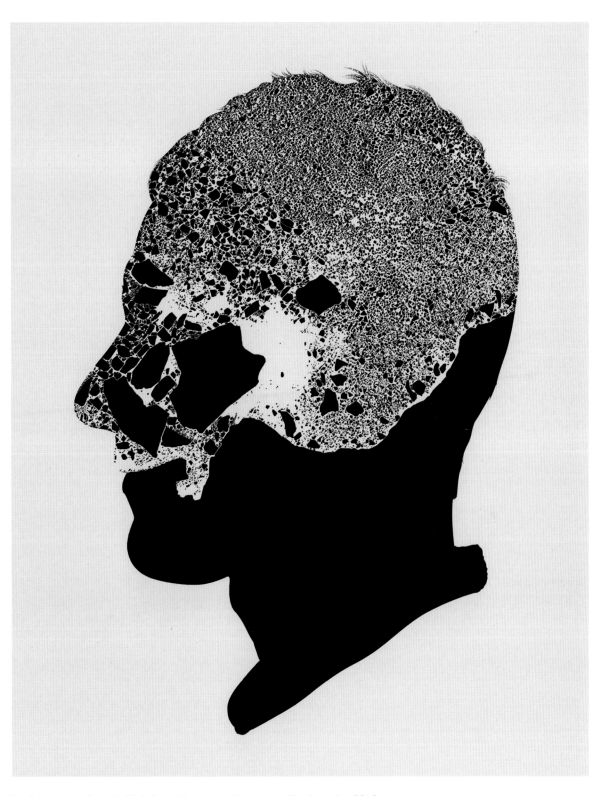

Vanish, personal work. Digital printing on matte paper with pigments, 2010.

Design of 150 posters with flags for a group exhibition of French heraldry, curated by Matthias Courtet and held during the III White Night of Metz.

Illustration published in the magazine *The Fader* for the association (RED), struggling to achieve that from 2015 no child is born with HIV.

Laboratório Secreto Design

Rio de Janeiro, Brazil
www.laboratoriosecreto.com

I'm Marcelo Martinez, a graphic designer and illustrator born in Rio de Janeiro, Brazil, in 1971. My studio, Laboratório Secreto, currently develops projects for both the cultural and publishing industries, as well as the advertising market. Some of our work was displayed and won awards in design, illustration and animation exhibitions in over 15 different countries all over the globe. Samples of our work were also printed in more than a dozen different publications such as Taschen's *Latin American Graphic Design*.

Different covers of novels designed between 2009 and 2011 for publishers such as Editora Record, Intrínseca, Agir, Editora Relume Dumará and Best Sellers.

Luis Sepúlveda

AUTOR DE *Um velho que lia romances de amor*

Diário de um killer sentimental

SEGUIDO DE

Jacaré

Relume Dumará

JORGE MAUTNER

O FILHO DO HOLOCAUSTO
MEMÓRIAS (1941 A 1958)

AGIR

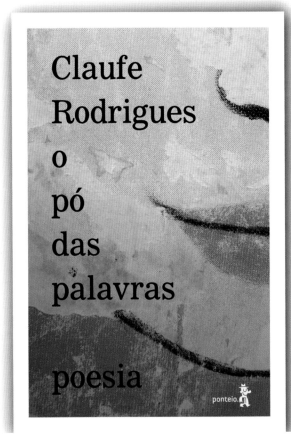

Claufe Rodrigues

o pó das palavras

poesia

ponteio.

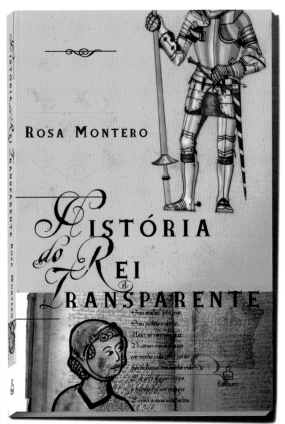

ROSA MONTERO

HISTÓRIA do REI TRANSPARENTE

Ediouro

1. *Vintage Rio* is a poster for the exhibition of the Society of Illustrators of Brazil held in Shanghai, China, in 2011.

2. *O Diário de um Mágico*, poster for the Irmãos Brothers show, a famous group of clowns and acrobats from Brazil.

PETROBRAS, OI, PREFEITURA DO RIO/CULTURAS APRESENTÂM

LABORATÓRIO SECRETO | ILUSTRAÇÃO DE MARCELO MARTINEZ

6º FESTIVAL INTERCÂMBIO DE LINGUAGENS

28 JUN_13 JUL.2008

TEATRO MUNICIPAL DO **JOCKEY** | TEATRO **JOÃO CAETANO**
OI FUTURO | CENTRO CULTURAL BANCO DO BRASIL/**CCBB**
TEATRO **TABLADO** | CAIXA CULTURAL/TEATRO **NELSON RODRIGUES**
TEATRO MUNICIPAL **MARIA CLARA MACHADO**

www.**fil**.art.br | REALIZAÇÃO TEATRO MUNICIPAL DO JOCKEY/ CENTRO MUNICIPAL DE REFERÊNCIA DO TEATRO INFANTIL

PATROCÍNIO

PARCERIA

PROMOÇÃO

APOIO

Illustration and poster for the 6th International Theatre Meeting for Young Audiences.

BON
EQUI
NHO
S VI
AJA
NTES

CLUBE DOS
PALHAÇOS

1. Poster and catalog for an exhibition by 84 Brazilian graphic artists held in 2010.

2-3. Logo design for children's clothing label Casa na Árbore, and a circus show, Clube dos Palhaços.

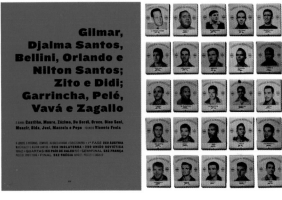

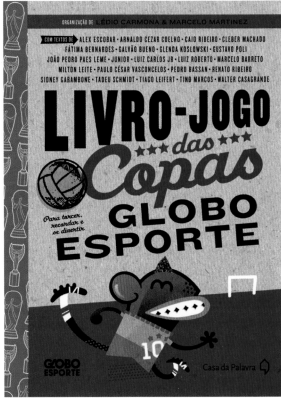

Livro-Jogo das Copas, published by Casa da Palavra publishers, is a project designed in 2010 for the World Cup. The book mixes humor, games, nostalgia and information, with the aim of making reading fun.

Design of several menswear catalogs for Father's Day or Valentine's Day for the label Toulon.

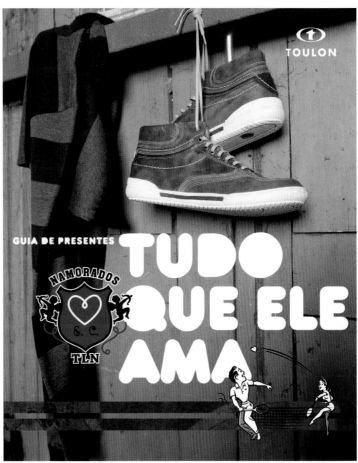

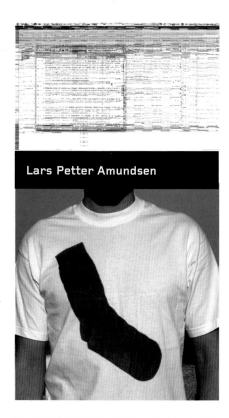

Lars Petter Amundsen

Santa Cruz de Tenerife, Spain
www.designbylars.com

I am a graphic designer living and working in Spain. I was born in Bergen (Norway) and studied at Central Saint Martin´s in London from 1995-2000. After graduating, I set up the studio Simon and Lars. Since 2008 I have worked for TEA Tenerife Espacio de las Artes (an art center designed by Herzog de Meuron). At the moment I am involved in several projects both in Spain and Norway. I am continually developing self-initiated projects to keep my thoughts and ideas as fresh as possibly. My main focus is the end-user of each project.

Winning design of the Tenerife Design Festival 2011. The theme was *Red and Blue*.

When the Japanese mend broken objects, they aggrandize the damage by filling the cracks with gold. They believe that when something's suffered damage and has a history it becomes more beautiful.

~Barbara Bloom

POSTERS FOR JAPAN
100ting til ettertanke

2011 © Siv Støldal & Lars Amundsen

Design of a poster in solidarity with Japan after the tsunami of 2011, which devastated the country's northern coast. The idea was developed in collaboration with fashion designer Siv Støldal, darning an old jersey.

TEA
tenerife espacio de las artes

17 nov 10 > 13 feb 11

COLECCIÓN TEA

EL CUERPO INVENTADO

TEA Tenerife Espacio de las Artes
Avda. San Sebastián 10
Santa Cruz de Tenerife

www.teatenerife.es

Graphic design for the exhibition *The Invented Body*, exhibited in the TEA, Tenerife Arts Space.

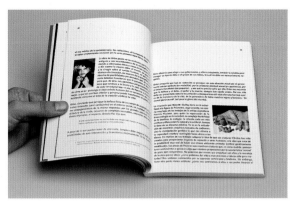

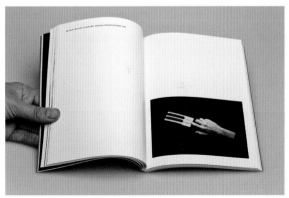

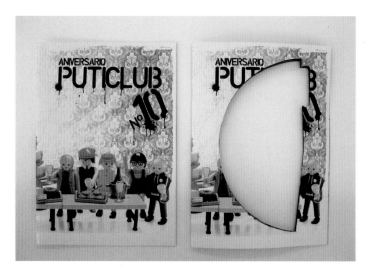

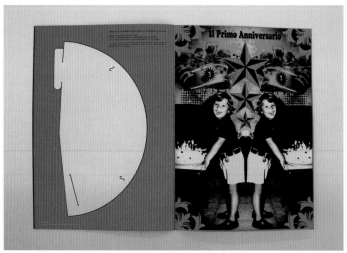

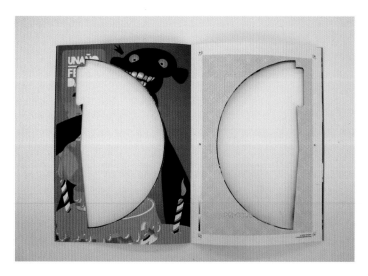

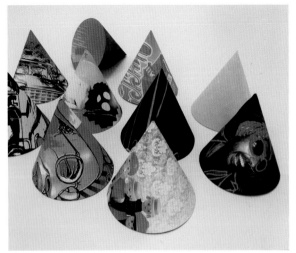

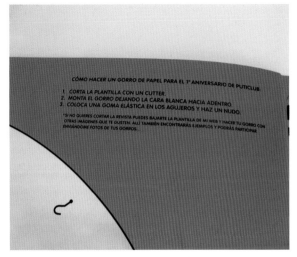

CÓMO HACER UN GORRO DE PAPEL PARA EL 1º ANIVERSARIO DE PUTICLUB:

1. CORTA LA PLANTILLA CON UN CUTTER.
2. MONTA EL GORRO DEJANDO LA CARA BLANCA HACIA ADENTRO.
3. COLOCA UNA GOMA ELÁSTICA EN LOS AGUJEROS Y HAZ UN NUDO.

*SI NO QUIERES CORTAR LA REVISTA PUEDES BAJARTE LA PLANTILLA DE MI WEB Y HACER TU GORRO CON OTRAS IMÁGENES QUE TE GUSTEN. ALLÍ TAMBIÉN ENCONTRARÁS EJEMPLOS Y PODRÁS PARTICIPAR ENVIÁNDOME FOTOS DE TUS GORROS.

Puticlub is a free magazine distributed in Spain. Design By Lars designed the edition for the first anniversary, the pages can be torn out to make typical paper birthday hat.

Léon & Loes

Rotterdam, the Netherlands
www.leon-loes.nl

Do

The
Imperative
Project

An interactive artwork that
examines the demands we make
of each other in public space

The Rotterdam-based design studio Léon & Loes specializes in transforming the abstractions of theory into powerful images. When research reaches an apex, and objects of study take shape, a space opens up for an image: a visual summary of the issues at hand. For us good design requires in-depth preparation and research of both theoretical and visual aspects of the object. The dynamics, and especially the playground between the sender and receiver, trigger and challenge us to change and manipulate the context. In this way, a setting is created, where we place the subject in a different context. Re-contextualizing theory, data, images and tangible materials, as well remixing and mixing this, results in a layered design; as well conceptual as visual, which sometimes can be comforting, sometimes exciting and sometimes in your face. It should always be well-thought through so the public and the message get the attention they deserve.

The Imperative Project examines the demands that are made in public space. The booklet, for example, is a demand in itself.

Brochure designed for the Dutch Designers Association to mark the conference *Food for Thought*.

The exposition *The Keys* connects a historic building in the city of Amsterdam with the stories of residents of the Frankendael house. Nine artists have carried out work that reflects on the past and present of this building.

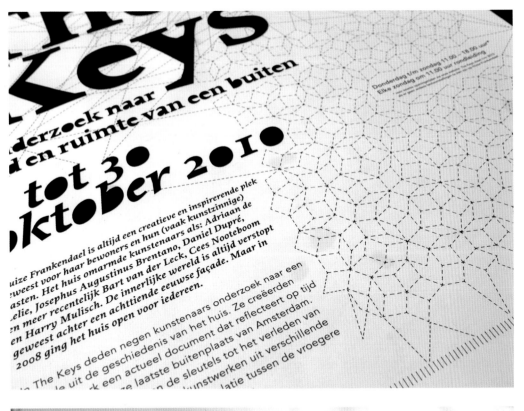

Léon & Loes designed the poster, the invitation and a publication for the exhibition. The laser cutting technique used for the poster can play with the concept of the quest for space and the idea of full and empty.

1-3. The designers came up with a few chairs in the form of bags of flour for the Year of the Mills in the Netherlands (2011). 70 people of different ages were involved in the project to share experiences and knowledge.

Towards a New Kind of Building

KAS OOSTERHUIS

A Designer's Guide for Nonstandard Architecture

NAi Publishers

Design of the architect Kas Oosterhuis monographic book, founder of the ONL studio. Posted by Nai Publishers.

Luis Urculo

Madrid, Spain
www.luisurculo.com

I studied at ETSAM (Madrid) and the Institute of Design in Chicago. I am interested in all that is peripheral to architecture, the processes, developments and approaches that can be manipulated, sampled and translated into other scales, adapting results to the composition of the project, creating new scenes/experiences/expectationsthat have not been contemplated previously. Our projects can take on diverse formats for clients including Philippe Starck, Absolut, Rolling Stone, Zara... where the barriers of the graphic and space language are questioned as something unique. They work as a whole. Currently, I live and work in Madrid.

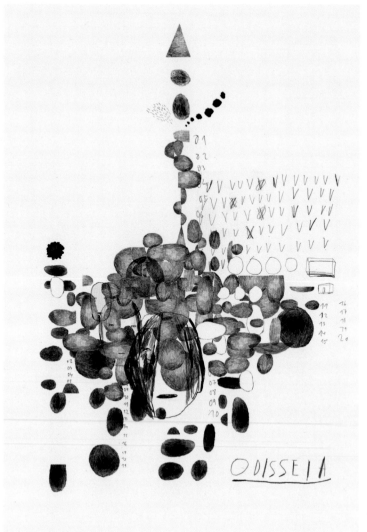

Design for the movie *Odisseia*, project selected by Julio Dolbeth project for the Festival Curtas.

Poster for the play by Metatarso Producciones *La vida imaginaria de Bonnie & Clyde*, directed by Dario Facal.

Art Direction, invitations and posters for the X Biennial of Architecture and Planning.

1. *Home* album cover, by the group Bing Ji Ling, edited by Lovemonk Records.

2. Illustrations for the Ramses, Madrid club and restaurant wine list by Philippe Stark.

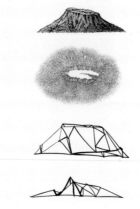

Diez album cover by Eliseo Parra. Three different covers
have been designed with combinations of three colors.

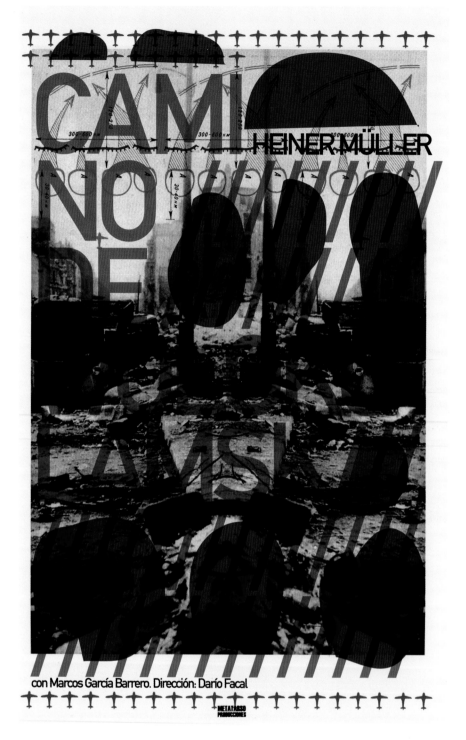

Poster for the play *Camino de Wolokolamsk*, by Heiner Müller, for Metatarso Producciones.

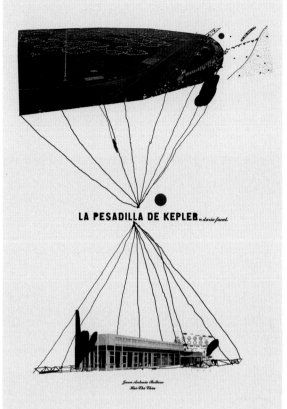

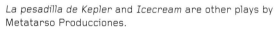

La pesadilla de Kepler and *Icecream* are other plays by Metatarso Producciones.

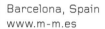

Barcelona, Spain
www.m-m.es

Marion Dönneweg and Merche Alca-
lá: What does a graphic designer and
an architect do together? After many
years of each working in their discipline, in late 2006 we decided to join
forces to test a new formula. We are
convinced that if you think of a project
together something coherent emerg-
es, from which one discipline builds on
the other. We eat breakfast together
and we share a table. Imagine what
an architect can see in a container or
a graphic designer on a wall. We try to
always have an emotional attachment
to the customer with the brand, and
this is not achieved only by decorat-
ing a space with the logo or corporate
colors, but it requires a more subtle
language. While we are excited about
the fusion of architecture and graphic
design, not all projects require it, so
both of us keep working in our own
discipline, and we love it.

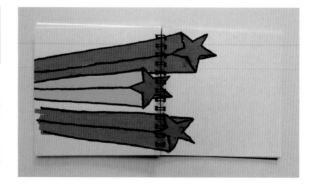

Corporate identity design for male underwear firm Jules
et Moi.

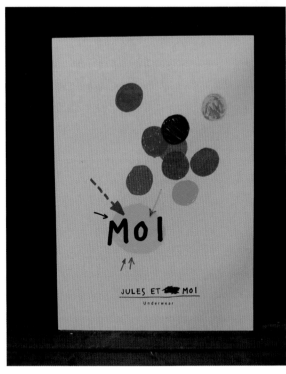

Composición:

100% ✚ happy pills

3% Azul cielo
5% Amarillo limon
2% Chiste verde
4% Humor negro
7% Carcajada descontrolada
8% La vie en rose
2% Cosquillas
7% Naranjas de la China
1% Fino humor British
2% Retranca gallega
6% Acento andaluz
9% Gol en el ultimo minuto
2% Esencia de amanecer
2% Ho ho ho
7% Algodón de Azúcar
3% Agujetas de reírse
Agu... les y a lo loco

For a candy store located in a tourist area, an adult image was designed, based on the idea that sweets provide small moments of happiness.

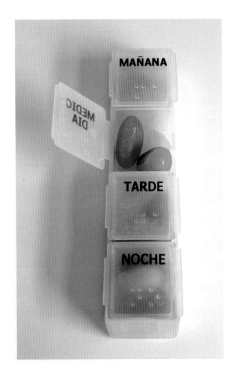

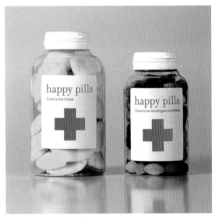

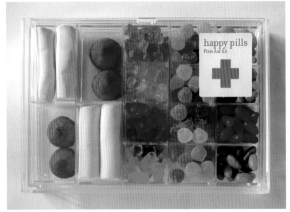

In addition to the interior design of the store, the studio designed the product concept, corporate identity and packaging of their products.

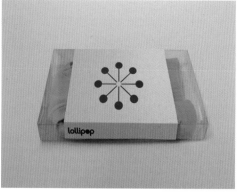
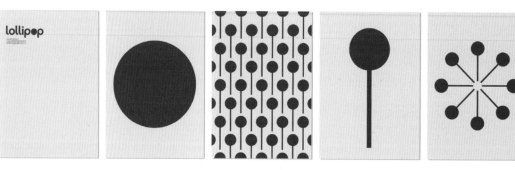
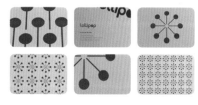
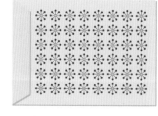

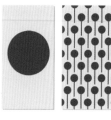

Corporate identity of the Lollipop children's clothing distribution company. The design suits the clothing line, which are modern and functional.

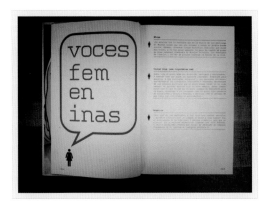

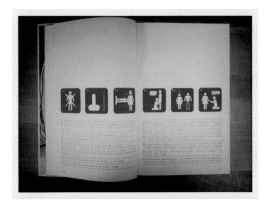

Concept and design of the porno book aimed at women *Porn for Women*, edited by Lust, the producer of adult entertainment by Erika Lust.

Maquinofobiapianolera/
13-16 oct

De Carles Santos y CaboSanRoque

Producción: CaboSanRoque y MOM / El Vivero

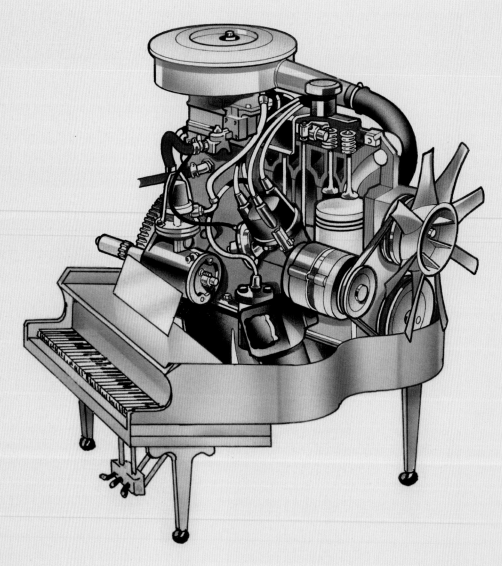

Juicio/ a/una/zorra/
02-20 nov

Texto y dirección: Miguel del Arco
Con: Carmen Machi

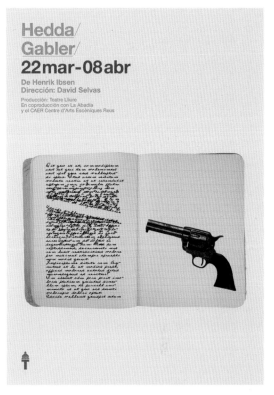

Hedda/ Gabler/
22 mar-08 abr

De Henrik Ibsen
Dirección: David Selvas

Producción: Teatre Lliure
En coproducción con La Abadía
y el CAER Centre d'Arts Escèniques Reus

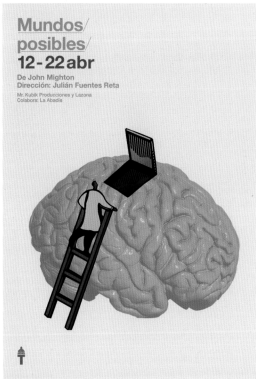

Mundos/ posibles/
12-22 abr

De John Mighton
Dirección: Julián Fuentes Reta

Mr. Kubik Producciones y Lazona
Colabora: La Abadía

Grooming/
01 feb -11 mar

De Paco Bezerra
Dirección: José Luis Gómez
Con: Nausicaa Bonnín y Antonio de la Torre
Producción: Teatro de La Abadía

Concept and design of posters and all communication artwork for plays at the Teatro de la Abadía, a theater house and studio dedicated to the creation and exhibition of theater shows.

**Mario Hugo
(Hugo & Marie)**

New York, NY, USA
www.mariohugo.com

Mario Hugo is a graphic designer and artist living in New York. Despite spending exorbitant amounts of time at the computer, he is someone who feels more true to himself when working with a brush and several sheets of paper in front of him. He has worked for major companies including Nike, Dolce & Gabbana, British Airways, EMI Music, MTV, Stella McCartney, ESP Institute, Granta, Portobello Books and Channel 4. Along with other designers, he forms part of the group Hugo and Marie (www.hugoandmarie.com).

Illustration *Cannibalism*, designed for an individual exhibition at the Vasava Gallery.

Design for *Modern Guilt*, eleventh album by the Californian musician Beck.

1. Art direction and illustration for *The Hazards of Love*, fifth album by the group The Decemberists.

2. Illustration for the cover of the magazine *Flaunt*, specializing in art, music, literature and fashion.

1. Illustration *Hope*, designed for a solidarity campaign.

2. Typography drawn with ink created for an album by the Norwegian artist Hanne Hukkelberg.

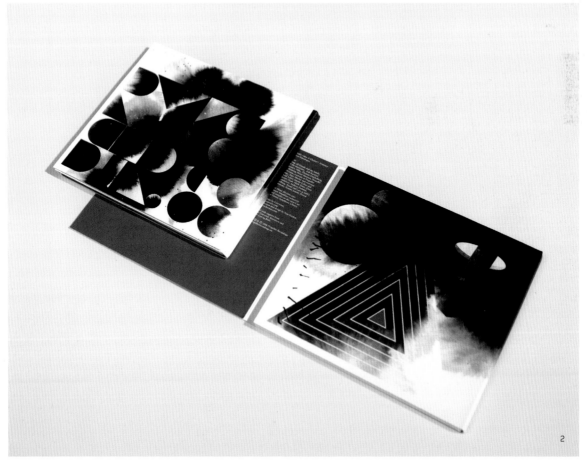

Inspirations is a typographic poster from a series designed for the company Microsoft.

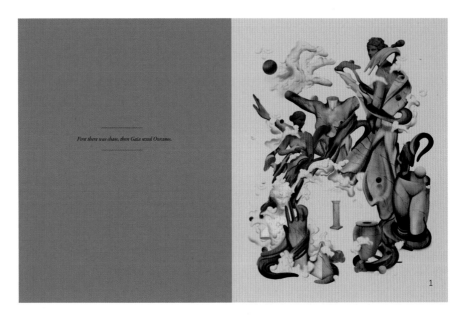

First there was chaos, then Gaia sexed Oaranus.

1. Illustration for the inside pages of the *The Love & Sex* issue of the magazine *Untitled*.

2. Illustration for the album cover by the folk artist J. Tillman *A Year in the Kingdom*.

TDC is the title of a typographic illustration created for the Type Director's Club of New York.

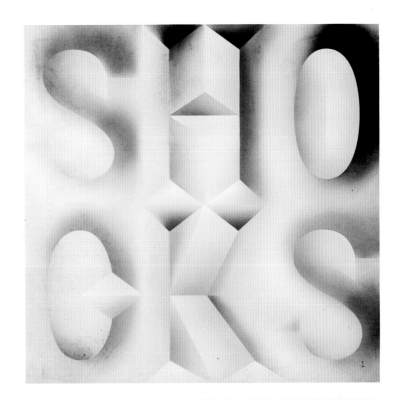

1. The Shocks album cover, created for the ESP Institute label.

2. *1502* is the title of an illustration designed for the entertainment and technology magazine *Wired*.

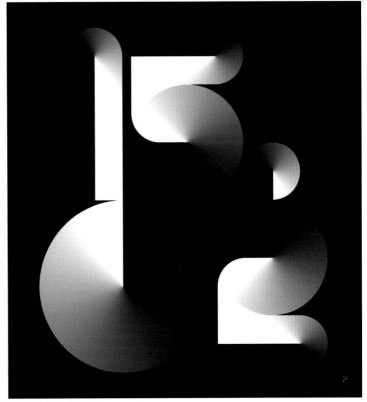

Martijn Oostra

Amsterdam, the Netherlands
www.martijnoostra.com

The difference between various creative occupations will be less clear in the future. More often designers are seen to be editors and designers of magazines and books or designer and artist at the same time. I work as a graphic designer, photographer, artist and publicist. My projects vary from video art to letter type design. There's a continuous thread in all my activities, whether it's a graphic design or an article that I wrote, it's is created with the tools by which I communicate. I find my tools in the media or in public areas (the street). One shows how daily life is coded. What is banal in one context becomes meaningful in another. I'm always looking for the beauty in triviality, but my work does have meaning, it's about what surrounds us.

Illustration for a magazine with food as the main theme.

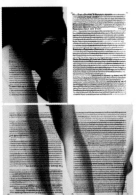

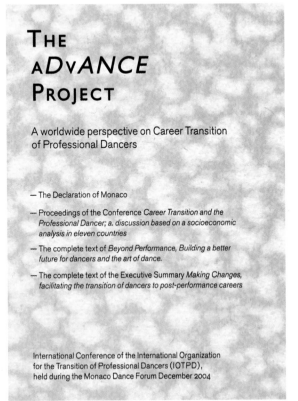

THE aDvANCE PROJECT

A worldwide perspective on Career Transition
of Professional Dancers

— The Declaration of Monaco

— Proceedings of the Conference *Career Transition and the
Professional Dancer; a. discussion based on a socioeconomic
analysis in eleven countries*

— The complete text of *Beyond Performance, Building a better
future for dancers and the art of dance.*

— The complete text of the Executive Summary *Making Changes,
facilitating the transition of dancers to post-performance careers*

International Conference of the International Organization
for the Transition of Professional Dancers (IOTPD),
held during the Monaco Dance Forum December 2004

THE aDvANCE PROJECT

A worldwide perspective on Career Transition
of Professional Dancers

— The Declaration of Monaco

— Proceedings of the Conference *Career Transition and the
Professional Dancer; a. discussion based on a socioeconomic
analysis in eleven countries*

— The complete text of *Beyond Performance, Building a better
future for dancers and the art of dance.*

— The complete text of the Executive Summary *Making Changes,
facilitating the transition of dancers to post-performance careers*

International Conference of the International Organization
for the Transition of Professional Dancers (IOTPD),
held during the Monaco Dance Forum December 2004

Report by the IOTPD organization. The photography by Joris-Jan Bos is shown fragmented on the interior.

Zem Zem

Tijdschrift over het Midden-Oosten, Noord-Afrika en islam   1 / 2008   € 8,-

60 jaar Nakba

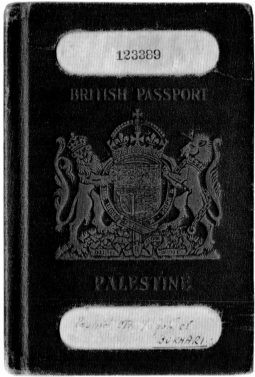

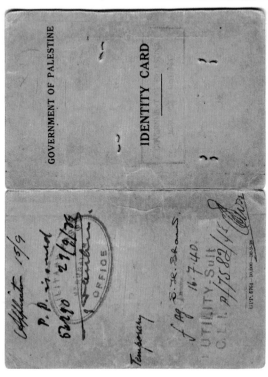

Cover for the German magazine *Zem Zem*, aimed at the Middle East, North Africa and Islam.

Illustrations designed for a personal scrapbook.

Series of postcards made from photographs of the designer.

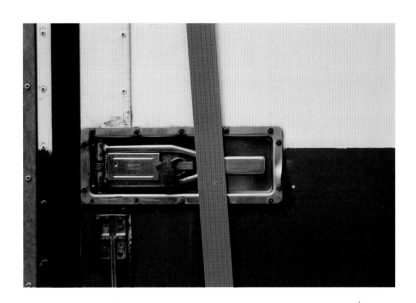

Merijn Hos
(Hugo & Marie)

Utrecht, the Netherlands
http://bfreeone.com

Merijn Hos, known under his alias "bfree", is an artist and illustrator from Utrecht, The Netherlands. He graduated with a BFA in Illustration in the School of Visual Arts of Utrecht (2004). He divides his time between working as a commercial illustrator and working on his own personal projects, exhibitions and independent publishing. Merijn's clients include Coca-Cola, Leifsdottir, *Wired Magazine*, *Vice Magazine*, Keds, Le Sportsac, Nickelodeon, and Nike. He has also participated in group and solo exhibitions.

Illustrations *Chapter 1* and *Chapter 2* created for an exhibition on the Genesis Group in the London art gallery Chapter One.

Design of an ad for an advertising campaign for Coca-Cola Europe.

1

2

3

1-2. Illustration of a series created for the exhibition *Don't Worry Be Happy*.

3. Poster for the Environmental Film Festival of Amsterdam.

Typographic illustration for a T-shirt with one of the most popular slogans of the sports label Nike.

Illustration for the association (RED), published in the magazine *The Fader*.

Commemorative poster for the creative agency Dixon Baxi, who invited 25 copywriters to work on the project.

Micah Lidberg
(Hugo & Marie)

Kansas City, MO, USA
http://micahlidberg.com

Micah is an illustrator based out of Kansas City. His experiences living in several parts of the US, as well as studying in Brighton, England, have contributed to his sincere love for practical design, bizarre phenomenon, and wonders of nature and travel. He works with a variety of media, often combining digital aspects to several types of illustration and painting. Micah adores pattern, color, and the notion that image-making is one of many straightforward and native modes of communication.

Illustrations created for the fourth issue of the magazine *Untitled Magazine*. Photography by James Mahon.

Design of a Nike poster for the special campaign *Sneak & Destroy*.

Design of the album covers and *Pink Graffiti* and *Strange Hearts* by the psychedelic pop group Secret Cities.

Typographic poster design. Above: poster for the band Phish. Below: illustration.

1. Poster *Nobrow Jungle*, for Nobrow Press.

2. Illustration that celebrates one year of illustrations for the spine of the Russian edition of *Esquire* magazine.

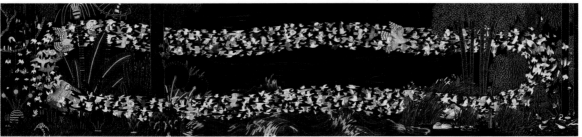

1. Cover of Book *A Graphic Cosmogony*, by Nobrow Press.

2. Design of three illustrations for Neenah Paper, paper manufacturer.

Michelle Sonderegger/
Design Ranch

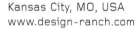

Kansas City, MO, USA
www.design-ranch.com

When I graduated from the University
of Kansas with a BFA, I hit the ground
running. I was lucky to have a hand
in shaping some big name brands like
Lee Jeans and Einstein Bros. Bagels
while working at Bagby Design, Muller
& Company and Willoughby Design. In
1998, my now business partner, In-
gred Sidie and I had a harebrained
idea to start our own design studio.
Our company was built entirely on one
client and a passion for our work. Design Ranch has since moved out of my
basement and onto bigger and better
things, but our passion for trailblaz-
ing design remains the same.

Catalogue for the jeanswear label Lee. The theme of the catalog, entitled
The Voyage, is the journey of the first American immigrants. The paper,
typography and embossing design of the cover are typical of that era.

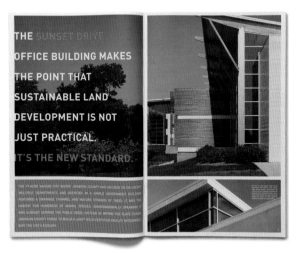

Corporate image for the 360 Architecture studio. The design and use of numbers in the name make the studio stand out in a professional field dominated by acronyms.

I CAN'T BELIEVE I HAVE TO SIT NEXT TO AUNT EDITH. IF SHE TRIES TO SPIT-CLEAN MY FACE ONE MORE TIME, I'LL SCREAM. WHEN DO I GET TO TAKE OFF THIS TIE? I HOPE MOM LETS ME DRINK SODA AT DINNER. I BET THE CAKE IS CHOCOLATE. IS THIS "I DO" STUFF OVER YET? THIS JACKET IS ITCHY. I'M READY TO BUST A MOVE AT THE RECEPTION. I'M GOING TO SHOW UNCLE CHARLIE MY NEW DANCE. I CALL IT THE "CRAZY TURTLE". I LOVE TURTLES.

Corporate image for the photographer Davis Tsai.

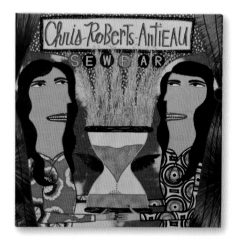

Book design for the exhibition of the textile artist Chris Roberts-Antieau in the Visionary Arts Museum in Baltimore.

The purpose of this catalog for the jeanswear label Lee was to address a young audience in a real-life way. The direct text and image support this communication channel.

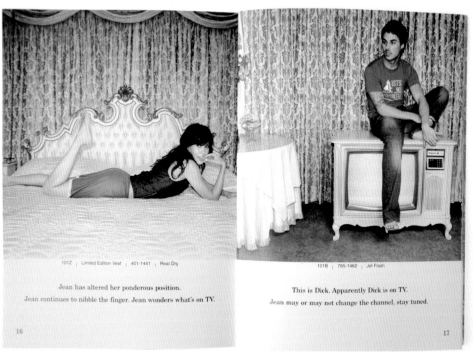

101Z | Limited Edition Vest | 401-1441 | Real Dry

Jean has altered her ponderous position.
Jean continues to nibble the finger. Jean wonders what's on TV.

101B | 785-1462 | Jet Flash

This is Dick. Apparently Dick is on TV.
Jean may or may not change the channel, stay tuned.

16

17

Catalog of the jeanswear label Lee with a vintage look as the main theme.

Masks from a line of accessories for Halloween parties by the label K&Company.

gum PHILOSOPHY No.09

Never miss a chance to have Sex or appear on television. —Gore Vidal

gum PHILOSOPHY No.10

ENJOY YOURSELF. IF YOU CAN'T ENJOY YOURSELF, ENJOY SOMEONE ELSE. —Jack Schaefer

gum PHILOSOPHY No.11

Better bread with water than cake with trouble.

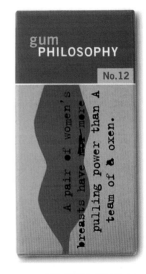

gum PHILOSOPHY No.12

A pair of women's breasts have more pulling power than a team of 8 oxen.

gum PHILOSOPHY No.01

things should be as SIMPLE as possible, but NO simpler.

gum PHILOSOPHY No.02

A GOOD PLAN TODAY IS BETTER THAN A PERFECT PLAN TOMORROW.

gum PHILOSOPHY No.03

It is better to go hungry than to get poisoned.

gum PHILOSOPHY No.04

LIFE IS SHORT, but WIDE.

gum PHILOSOPHY No.08

IT IS EITHER EASY OR IMPOSSIBLE —Salvador Dali

gum PHILOSOPHY No.06

Remember that the most Beautiful things in LIFE are also the most USELESS. PEACOCKS and LILIES for instance. —John Ruskin

gum PHILOSOPHY No.05

ART IS IN LOVE with LUCK, and LUCK with ART. —Graham Greene

gum PHILOSOPHY No.07

i am only a Public Entertainer WHO HAS understood HIS TIME. —Pablo Picasso

Design of gum boxes for Blue Q. The designer created the illustrations and calligraphy reproducing famous quotations about life.

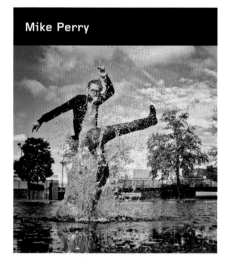

Mike Perry

New York, NY, USA
www.mikeperrystudio.com

As a designer and artist working in a
variety of mediums, including—but not
limited to—books, magazines, newspapers, clothing, drawing, painting,
and illustration, Mike Perry is com-
pelled by the ways in which hand-
drawn formats inform and deepen
contemporary visual culture. Perry
works regularly for a number of editorial and commercial clients including Apple, *The New York Times*, Dwell,
Target, Urban Outfitters, eMusic, and
Nike. In 2004, he was chosen as one
of *Step* magazine's 30 under 30, and,
in 2007, as a *Groundbreaking Illustrator* by Computer Arts Projects. In
2008, he received *Print* magazine's
New Visual Artist Award. His work
has been exhibited around the world
including the two recent, solo shows
in Tokyo, Japan, *We are the Infinity of
Each Other* at B Gallery and *Color,
Shapes and Infinity* at Public/Image.
3D Gallery.

Illustration for the cover of the Magazine *Grafik*, a publication
specializing in graphic design.

Colored cedar slat sculpture created for the exhibition
Colab held in Australia.

1. Illustration for an announcement of the Cultural Institute of New York 92nd Street Y.

2. Treatment of the logo for Accept + Proceed.

Illustration for an advertisement in music, art, culture and trends magazine *The Fader*.

1. Advertisement created for the association (RED).

2. Design of a logo for Nike 6.0.

3. Illustration of an ampersand for the New York 2010 Fashion Week runway show which brought together the cosmetics company MAC and the fashion label Milk.

Design of a typographic ad for the city of New York entitled *This Is NYC*.

Poster of the band Sleater Kinney, designed for Insound Classics.

Personal abstract work.

Mimi

Buenos Aires, Argentina
www.holamimi.com

Mimi is the professional name of Mek Frinchaboy designer from Buenos Aires, Argentina. She studied graphic design at the University of Buenos Aires, where she graduated with honors. In this university, she taught classes in Enrique Longinotti's typography courses for four years. Since childhood, she has had a keen passion for colors and letters, two elements that are always present in her work. She currently works as a freelance graphic designer as well as an editorial illustrator.

1. Illustration for article *Cuando el vino es verde* from the Argentinean magazine *El Gourmet*.

2. Illustration for the article *Alimentos grandiosos que te estás perdiendo*, from the web www.tualmazen.com.

Calligraphy and illustration for BHDM (Basehead Digital Media), design studio specializing in digital and interactive media.

Different calligraphic illustrations for T-shirts from the child clothing label Chibel.

Design of calligraphy, illustration and embroidery for the wedding of Thais and Nicolas.

Serigraphs for applications such as illustrations, books and postcards. Chocho Project: www.estoychocho.com.ar.

Illustration for T-shirts from the children's clothing label Chibel.

Illustration for clothing and web applications for the children's label Giocare.

MVM (Hugo & Marie)

Drammen, Norway
http://themvm.com

MVM is a graphic design studio established by Norwegian graphic designer and illustrator Magnus Voll Mathiassen in 2009. Magnus was a co-founder of the studio Grandpeople, which received worldwide design acclaim. Magnus currently works on illustration, graphic design, and art direction projects for clients such as Neenah Paper, Microsoft Zune, Nike, Bergen International Festival, MTV Nordic, Converse, and *Varoom Magazine*. MVM focuses on research-driven work. A strong conceptual foundation is important to secure strong aesthetics. Both commercial and non-commercial work are equally regarded as important fields of exploration.

PMU Linda is an illustration belonging to a series of large-scale works created for the annual graphic design trade show *Pick Me Up*, held at Somerset House in London.

Poster designed by MVM, from the Hugo & Marie collection, for an advertising campaign for Nike Europe.

Several illustrations. The first is a study based on the faces of Jean Arp. The second, an illustration created for the fashion project *Borders* & *Frontiers*.

Illustration *Else in Love*.

Illustrations pertaining to a series that portrays various rap stars. Left: portrait of JayZ. Right: image of Snoop Dogg.

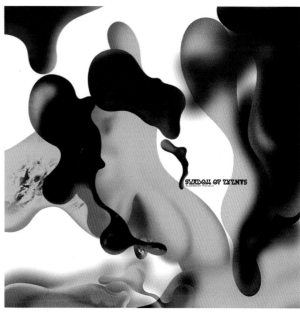

Above: illustration created for the group Hugo & Marie, of which the designer forms part. Below: design of cover of the Alexander Rishaug album *Shadow of Events*.

MY.S

São Paulo, Brazil
www.my-sss.com

We are a graphic design & illustration studio based in São Paulo, established in 2007. The studio was formed as a result of the partnership and friendship between two graphic designers, Maíra Fukimoto and Yara Fukimoto, and the fashion designer Stephanie Marihan. We love doing beautiful things and we think design is the source for helping people and nature to be balanced and more integrated. We also have fun at work, so that's the reason for creating and developing some first-class work.

The work that the designers created for a group exhibition was a bench, which reflected on the individualism of modern society. Digital artwork on plywood. Dimensions: 100 x 100 x 45 cm.

Design of patterns for promotional use in videos and promotions of the *Boomerang Channel* in Latin America.

Illustrations and design of a 2012 calendar for the company TEKA Stationery.

JANEIRO

D	S	T	Q	Q	S	S
1	2	3	4	5	6	7
8	9	10	11	12	13	14
15	16	17	18	19	20	21
22	23	24	25	26	27	28
29	30	31				

ABRIL

D	S	T	Q	Q	S	S
1	2	3	4	5	6	7
8	9	10	11	12	13	14
15	16	17	18	19	20	21
22	23	24	25	26	27	28
29	30					

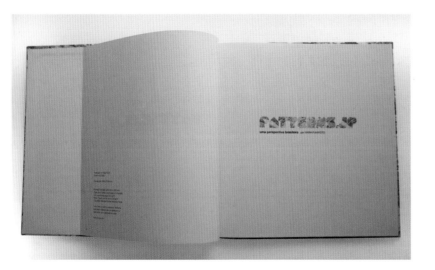

Design of a book that represents the flora and fauna of Brazil. The illustrations are by half Japanese, half Brazilian designer, showcasing the mixture of these two cultures in the design.

ALÊ ABIURO

ESTÚDIO ÁRVORE

ESTÚDIO ÁREA

ESTÚDIO CAMPO

ESTÚDIO COLLETIVO

GRAFIK

abertura 18/12/10
16hrs
cartel 011
r. artur de
azevedo, 517
pinheiros/sp

a expo
definitiva
do
design
gráfico

ELLEN TONIATTI

EDGAR DE CAMARGO

MARCELO ARNOLD

MY.S

PRISCILA GURSKI

RICARDO DE CASTRO

CURADORIA: CACÁ DI GUGLIELMO
ORGANIZAÇÃO: CARTEL 011
PATROCÍNIO: DIGITAL PRINT
ILUSTRAÇÃO: MY.S

The eleven designers of the group exhibition *Grafik* had to work with vinyl as support. The studio MY.S dealt with the issue of interactivity and permitted spectators to change their work.

Naroska Design

Berlin, Germany
www.naroska.de

Corporate Design Berlin Music Week, one of the important musical events of the German capital.

Marc Naroska studied visual communication at the Potsdam University of Applied Sciences. Since 1999, he has been working under his own name on national and international design projects. Naroska's design studio is specialized in corporate images, company publications, books, magazines, exhibitions, orientation systems, and web applications. His experience with design projects for customers like Michael Michalsky, the Helmut Newton Foundation, the Norwegian Ministry of Foreign Affairs, and SantaVerde Natural Products. Marc Naroska is founder and partner of C/O Berlin, an exhibition center that has been presenting a lively cultural program of international stature.

Large signage and exhibition design for the famous
classical music label Deutsche Grammophon.
Photography by www.harfzimmermann.com.

Mies
125

1886–2011 **125 JAHRE**
MIES VAN DER ROHE

Logo and poster design for the Mies van der Rohe exhibition to mark the 125th anniversary of his birth.

Editorial design for Gregory Crewdson's photography book, published by Hatje Cantz Publishers.

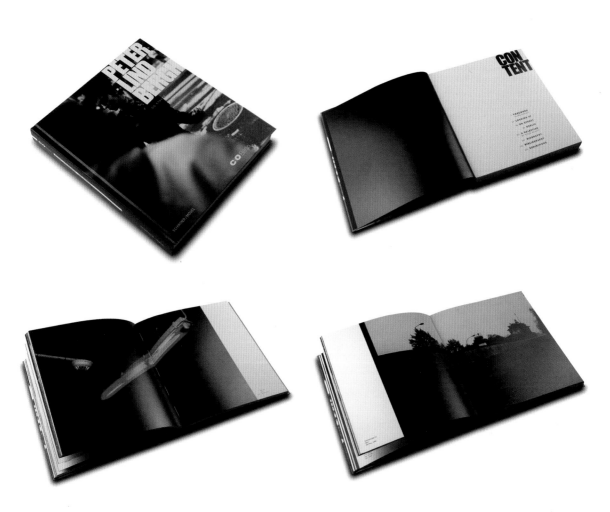

Editorial design for photographer Peter Lindbergh, published by Schirmer / Mosel and C/O Berlin, the organization founded by the designer Marc Naroska.

Nathalie Fallaha

Beirut, Lebanon
www.vit-e.com, www.alephya.com

I am the founder and catalyst behind Vit-e design studio. I studied graphic design at the American University of Beirut; after receiving my bachelor of Graphic Design in 1997, I moved to Central Saint Martins in the UK to pursue my Masters in Communication Design. I was awarded the *Lebanese Design Entrepreneur of the Year* in 2008 by the British Council. My work has been published in several international books, magazines, and publications. Passionate about bilingual typography (Arabic-Latin), most of my personal work is driven by the urge to explore the expressive power of the letterforms on different substrates. Vit-e is a multi-disciplinary design studio working in many facets of branding, visual identity, art direction, packaging, print and interactive design. We have the experience and knowledge of a big creative agency combined with the personal touch of a boutique studio.

Design of logo, image and website for this online clothing and accessories store of designers in the Arab world. It was voted one of the best fashion websites in the world by *Financial Times* in June 2010.

Design of graphics, corporate image and menus for restaurant 365, in Beirut, Lebanon.

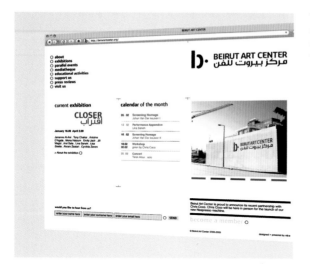

The Beirut Art Center, a nonprofit organization and cultural and artistic space, held a contest for the brand design, publishing house, web and design of spaces. The winner was the studio vit-e.

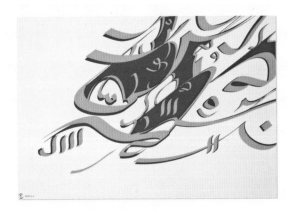

The designs for the brand Alephya originate from
an aesthetic that unites Arabic calligraphy and the
Arabesques.

Roundtable is a personal piece of work which attempts
to make an experimental trip towards multilingualism.
Documents with typographical elements gather views on
the use of language and national identity.

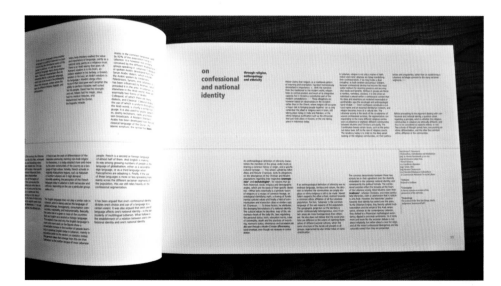

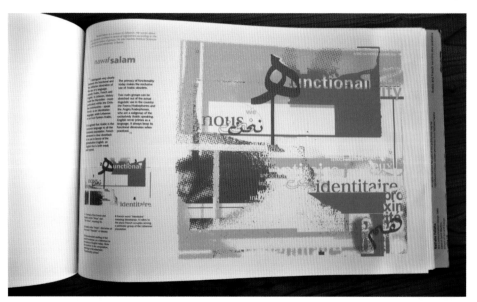

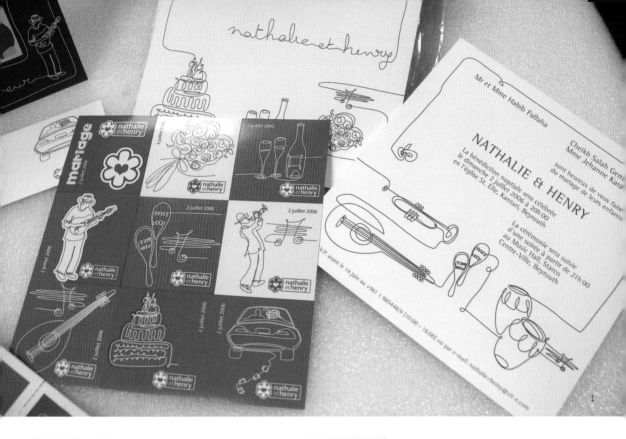

1. *Kit Bonheur* is the design of the packaging and invitations to the designer's wedding.

2. Logo design, branding, menu and website for Kitsch, a cupcake company.

Concept, design and programming of a series of e-gadgets for Google Middle East iGoogle.

Niessen & de Vries

Amsterdam, the Netherlands
www.niessendevries.nl

We are Niessen (Richard, born in Edam-Volendam in 1972) & de Vries (Esther, born in The Hague in 1974). We describe our work as 'lyrical design': expressive and imaginative, using a richer language to appeal to the senses and the intellect. Our work is involved, subjective and personal in origin. It is spontaneous, even conversational, not intended to impress with its erudition or cleverness. The fact that we are graphic designers doesn't limit us to two dimensions or sole print work: our designs range from exhibitions to textiles and from ceramics to coins, always highly compressed allowing to unfurl the meaning.

Initiative of the Niessen & de Vries designers to research the foundations of graphic design and printing as a form of artistic expression. Brochures and posters are inspired by the work of several artists, musicians and designers.

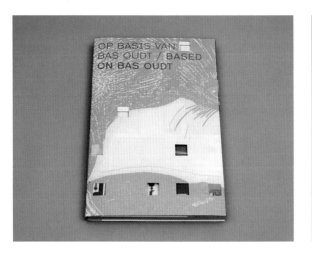

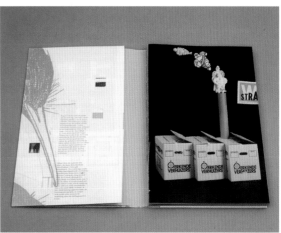

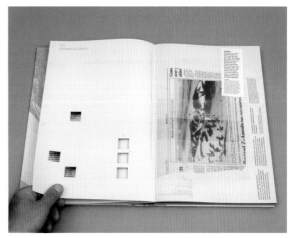

Commemorative volume for Bas Oudt, graphic designer, typographer and teacher. It was published by De Buitenkant in 2009, in English and Dutch.

This poster was created for the textile company Maharam from images of entrances to houses on the island of Samos, made by the designers themselves.

Poster designed in 2008 to celebrate the 70th anniversary of the French train company SNCF. The slogan *Donner au train des idées d'avance* should appear on the poster.

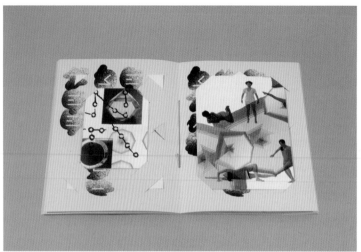

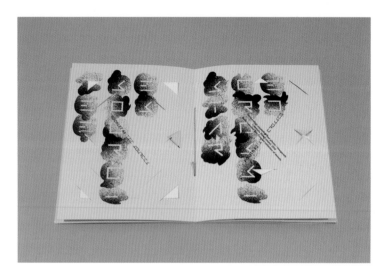

2010 publication of the exhibition by the artist Jennifer Tee in the space
Eastside Projects.

376

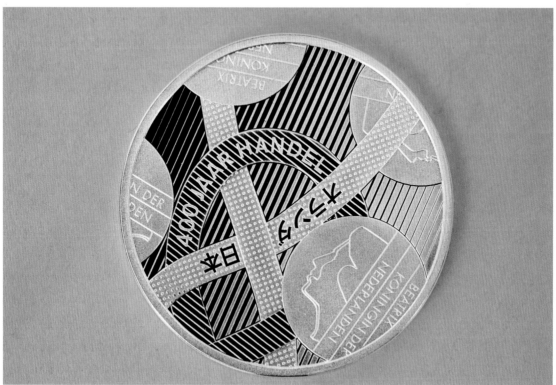

Design of a coin commemorating 400 years of trade relations between Japan and the Netherlands.

Design of a publication that becomes a small nest and serves to promote the traveling exhibition *Nest / Nester* by the artist Auke de Vries.

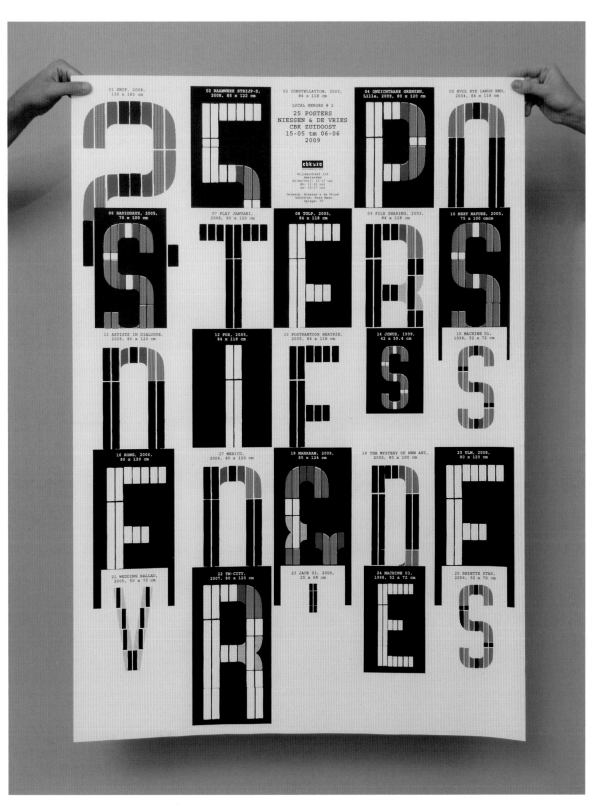

Poster for a poster exhibition. Each of the posters displayed is a letter in the poster, which also indicates the measurements and the title of each piece of work.

Nous Vous

London / Leeds, UK
www.nousvous.eu

Nous Vous is a collective working on design projects and educational programs. Image-making is central to our work. We have a bold, graphic visual language suited to a range of applications such as illustration, print design, animation and digital media, and we always attempt to imbue our work with a sense of positivity. We're interested in exploring new processes, working towards the most appropriate outcome for each project. We explore our collaborative practice most distinctly in the form of group demonstrations and improvised installations.

Posters designed at the request of the Contemporary Art Society of London for the Aspen offices.

Gallery

Forest

Exhibition

Maze

The promotional material was designed for the event
Light Night Leeds 2009/2010 commissioned by Leeds
City Council.

```
N G A T L O P E B I P O T D
E G H O T R A I D U L O N U
A P R O J E U T S I N S O N
D O T S S I O N B E C T K G
S C U L P T U R E L A R A E
N C T I O N A I R O K A L O
O P E A T R A K S E A L E N
I T S P Y B U D A L O B I K
T R A U T F E E R L U N D S
C O C R U T R A I N E N O D
E S D O S O N P R I B A S B
J U B I P O L A R F R U C I
O B I O N G N S E C A T O L
R B C H I N G G A F E C P T
P T R E C T U N S O N D E B
```

BEAR, FACE	KALEIDOSCOPE
PROJECTION	LIBRARY
GHOST	DUNGEON
SONGS	BIPOLAR
TRAIN	SCULPTURE

78 / The Light: Arts and Minds
The Light, LS1 8TL / 5.30pm-9pm
Arts and Minds explores the link between creativity and mental health. The annual exhibition will be on show and you will get the opportunity to meet some of the artists and contribute to a big communal artwork. Also featuring the Time to Change Tepee - come along to find out more!

79 / Bring The Happy: Invisible Flock
The Light, LS1 8TL / 5-11pm
'Bring the Happy' is an interactive shop where interactive arts trio Invisible Flock set to map the happiness of the people of Leeds over a six week period. Come and see their giant map, read the stories others have left and tell them how happy you are. Find out more and how you can participate at www.bringthehappy.co.uk

80 / Camp Angelic Shadow: Edward Mortimer
Holy Trinity Church, Boar Lane,
LS1 6HW / 5-11pm
This mythical angel is derived from archetypes in Italian Baroque statuary, classic male movie stars, and video gaming type figures. Expressive use of wire and mixed materials for spatial and theatrical effect and lighting the figure to distort unusual winter shadows suggests a slightly dark side to the camp.

81 / 'Lecimy' and other works.
Leeds Shopping Plaza, Top Floor,
LS1 5ER / 5-9pm
Chris Bloor and Graham Hibbert present a screening of abstract film and video works, created, using analogue and digital processes including minimalist sound composition, within the tradition of experimental film and expanded cinema.

82 / Animated Yorkshire hits Light Night!
Leeds Shopping Plaza, Top Floor,
LS1 5ER / 6.30-9pm
Animators from all over Yorkshire descend on a Leeds shop unit and light it up with fantastic projections! Come and add your contribution to our animation and find out more about the work of Animated Yorkshire. No previous experience needed

83 / The Beads of Leeds: Michelle Buckley/Orchid Artworks
St. John the Evangelist Church,
New Briggate, LS2 8JD / 6.30-10pm
An exciting new installation inside St. John's church. Thousands of beads will form a kaleidoscope of colours, light and shadow. The idea was borne from Light Night itself - the beads represent the diverse inhabitants of Leeds, while the frame symbolises the connectors created by Light Night to make something amazing happen. Bring some beads and your imagination!

**Name these
Leeds Landmarks**

1. 2. 3.
4. 5. 6.

1. ....
2. ....
3. ....
4. ....
5. ....
6. ....

28 / Swarthmore Shines
Swarthmore Adult Education Centre,
LS3 1AD / 6-9pm
Take part in creativity, dance and history at Swarthmore as part of 2010 Light Night. The spotlight this year is on taking part — in creativity, dance and history. Interactive Belly Dancing sessions, Swarthmore history tours and creating a unique piece of art that will depict the word SHINE!

29 / Cairn: Louisa Parker
Cairns at Park Square, Victoria Gdns,
Civic and Town Halls / 5-12pm
A memorial to the simple act of passing through, look for the glowing stones around the Light Night route, carry them awhile, feel the weight in your pocket and when the time has come to part, add a glowing stone to the Cairns that are growing around you. Monumental Cairn -Park Square, three small Duckies at Victoria Gardens chess board, Town Hall steps, Civic Hall steps.

30 / The Den Project
Park Square, LS1 2NY / 5-9pm
The Den Project will be building a temporary installation at Park Square in collaboration with children from two Leeds primary schools. In response to architectural features in the city the children will work with found, recycled, lightweight materials and light which will be built into a magical construction that visitors can get inside and explore.

31 / Ghost Train: People in Action
Oxford Chambers, Oxford Place,
LS1 3AX / 5-11pm
Step back in time with People in Action's unique walking ghost train. Listen to bone chilling ghost stories, buy wares from Victorian street sellers or browse the momento mori gallery. A piece of site specific, interactive theatre fun for all the family. Not to be missed!

32 / Flocks: Pyramid of Arts
Between Town Hall and Leeds Methodist Mission, Oxford Place,
LS1 3AX / 6-10.30pm
Happy Birthday Pyramid of Arts! Celebrate 21 years of inclusive arts projects with 'Flocks', a reflective installation of portraits, aerial sculptures, sound and sheep. Bring your decorated bird on the night and artists with and without learning disabilities will help you to add it to the flock. Watch out — sheep can stray.
Visit www.pyramid-of-arts.org.uk to join in.

33 / Town Hall Clock Tower Tour
The Town Hall, LS1 3AD / 5.30pm, 6.30pm, 7.30pm, 8.30pm, 9.30pm and 10.30pm
Your chance to climb the 203 steps for an opportunity to see inside the most iconic tower on the city's skyline, to see the movement of the clock that has marked Leeds' time for 150 years and 80,000,000 ticks. Access to the tower is by stairs only. Limited places available. Book at Town Hall on the night.

**1 / Waiting for the Winter:
Knit a Bear Face**
Various city centre statues around City Square, Dortmund Square, Bond Court and Victoria Gardens
4.30-11pm
Come and see the statues of Leeds wrapped up in winter knits. Each piece was knitted by Leeds knitting group 'Knit a Bear Face', and conjures up a part of the historic figure's past or a newly imagined scene, as well as keeping out the cold!

2 / Party Time: A Nod & A Wink
Outside several Light Night venues throughout the evening / 5-11pm
It's Party Time! So join A Nod & A Wink's interactive miniature parties all held on one large rug. This interactive piece pops up around the city. Don a feather boa and boogie like Swayze...Sip on a sombrero and salsa like Swayze...The party never stops...

3 / Harvesters: Urban Harvest
Peripatetic / 8-10pm
Look out for the wandering "harvesters" with their musical fruit cart full of surprises. Enter their weird and wonderful world, savour rich, flavoursome locally grown fruit, and then continue on your way with a keepsake to remind you of the wonders of local harvesting and growing.

**4 / Travelling Photo Booth:
Picture Fantastique**
Following the Light Night crowds!
5-10pm
Picture Fantastique's Amazing Travelling Photo Booth aims to put the spotlight back on the audience. Using glow sticks, pretty lights and long exposure techniques, the participants will create an artwork of their own that they can later download and keep. Find it in various locations over the night!

5 / Urban Nymphs: Rachel Slee, Sam Musgrove and Chemaine Cooke.
Round and about / 5-11pm
Amid the streets they live and lurk. Through daylight, moonlight, and streetlight, they touch, feel, taste, smell, look, listen, to the city And tonight you will meet them, framing all that is beautiful, interesting, curious, and brilliant around Leeds — including you.

**6 / Little Big Bang:
Katrien Van Liefferinge**
Participating Light Night venues throughout the evening / from 6pm
Share in the wishes and reflections created by the residents of Little Woodhouse in this collaborative artwork with artist in residence Katrien Van Liefferinge. Collect one of the 100 messages contained in your limited edition fortune cookie from various locations throughout Little Woodhouse and the city centre ...'the time is right to make new friends!' ...
LittleBigBang.blogspot.com

Promotional material for the event *MashUp* organized by the Institute of Contemporary Arts in London (ICA).

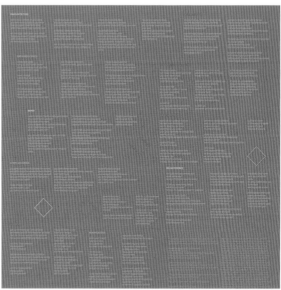

Design of the image and Tokyo Police Club album, commissioned by Tokyo Police Club and Mom & Pop Records.

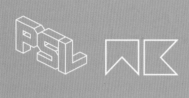

Morphic Resonance
25 March – 27 June 2009
Private View 12 May, 6-8pm

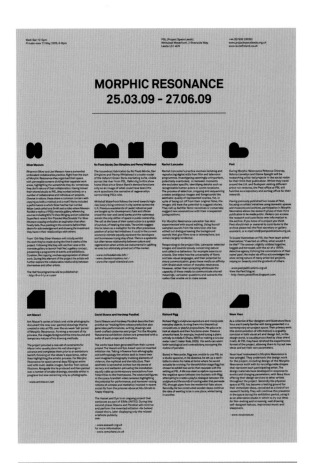

Promotional material for the exposition *Morphic Resonance*, organized by PSL (Project Space Leeds).

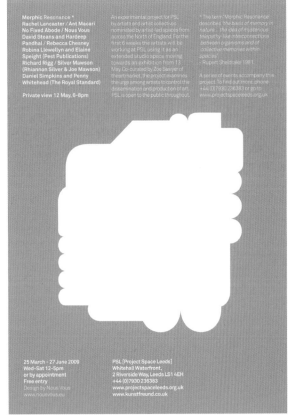

Oded Ezer

Givatayim, Israel
www.odedezer.com

I am a commercial graphic and type designer. I studied at the Bezalel Academy of Art & Design, Jerusalem. In 2000, I decided to set up my own independent studio, Oded Ezer Typography, in Givatayim, where I specialize in brand identity, typographic design and Hebrew and Latin typeface design. In 2004, I founded EzerFamily.com type foundry, selling my own typefaces. Some of my designs have been awarded local and international accolades and some of my projects, posters and graphic works are showcased and published worldwide, and form part of permanent collections of eminent museums such as the New York Museum of Modern Art (MoMA), Israel Museum of Art, Jerusalem, and the Museum für Gestaltung Zürich (Switzerland). My first monograph *Oded Ezer: The Typographer's Guide to the Galaxy* was published by Die Gestalten Verlag in May 2009.

1. The experimental typography Mohawk pays clear homage to the punk movement.

2. The project *1:3 1:5 1:7*, consisting of a poster and a video, was commissioned by Shufuni Shoes Fair for a charity exhibition for a center for victims of sexual assault.

The *Ketubah* is a traditional Jewish prenuptial agreement which sets down the obligations of the bridegroom to the bride. It is also one of the predominant forms of Jewish art.

פ ס אֶבְגָדֹה
אד פֹנְט
פ ס העברית א
פ ס א
פ ס גופנים א
פ ס א
פ ס פונט א

הופך מתפתל ומגיש לך פונט מטא עברית
קשורה בצרור עוצב על ידי עודד עזר
תנודות אוויר ריקות מלמעלה עבור פונטשופ אינטרנשיונל ברלין
כעץ בחורשה מבודדת. נישא גבוה מעל חבריו כוֹלֵל נִקוּד מָלֵא
צֹאן בַּרְזֶל טיפוגרפיה
הצייר סביבו מתהפכת היצירה אנציקלופדיה, עברית,
גדול משוררי הארץ תנ"ך וספרות
צבעים מוזיקליים רבים, דובני גריזלי כְּעֵץ שֶׁגָּדַל בְּיַעַר
שלום עליכם אהבת אמת
ועֹל כל עם ישראל

Typography is the main work area by Oded Ezer, whether it is experimental or a catalog of typefaces.

390

This design refers to the famous logo I ❤ NY, the work of Milton Glaser.

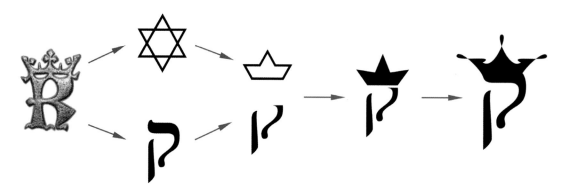

פסטיבל
התרבות
היהודית
בקרקוב

Festiwal
Kultury
Żydowskiej
w Krakowie

Festiwal
Kultury
Żydowskiej
w Krakowie

Jewish
Culture
Festival
Krakow

Festiwal
Kultury
Żydowskiej
w Krakowie

Jewish
Culture
Festival
Krakow

This poster and logo was designed for the Festival of Jewish Culture in Krakow. The fusion of symbols creates the logo, which is combined with different languages. The faces of the poster are related to new communication technologies.

+ ABC + ∞ =

Designing a tattoo is not a normal task for a typographer. This client wanted the initials of the names of his grandparents to be incorporated into the tattoo. The result evokes a timeline and infinity.

587 BCE

Jerusalem is conquered and destroyed by the army of Babylon, and the Israelites are taken captive as slaves. They live in forced exile for about 50 years, until king Cyrus the Great permits them to return home in 538.

500 BCE

The world's Jewish population is approximately 150,000, or about 2% of the total global population.

Dip it into salt-water and eat only a little bit.
(some follow the costume to recline/lean here too.)

Yahatz יַחַץ

Break the middle matzo into two. Wrap the larger part and set it aside, to be eaten towards the end of the seder. This is the Afikoman. A popular customs to hide it and have the children search for it later. The smaller piece is put back between the two whole matzo. Some place the afikoman briefly on their shoulders to reenact the Israelites' posture when fleeing Egypt.

Magid מַגִּיד

Karpas כַּרְפַּס

Dip a small piece of a vegetable in salt water and keeping the Maror in mind, and recite:

You are blessed, Lord and God-of-us, King of the Cosmos, who creates the earth's harvest.

בָּרוּךְ אַתָּה יי אֱלֹהֵינוּ מֶלֶךְ הָעוֹלָם,
בּוֹרֵא פְּרִי הָאֲדָמָה.

023   022

1542

In winter, Paulus von Eitzen, bishop of Schleswig, attends church in Hamburg and claims to see a barefoot man with long hair and ragged clothing, who beats his chest whenever the name of Jesus was spoken. He claims that he is a shoemaker named Ahasuerus, and that he had cursed Jesus before his martyrdom.

וַיּוֹצִאֵנוּ יהוה מִמִּצְרַיִם. לֹא עַל יְדֵי מַלְאָךְ וְלֹא עַל יְדֵי שָׂרָף
וְלֹא עַל יְדֵי שָׁלִיחַ, אֶלָּא הַקָּדוֹשׁ בָּרוּךְ הוּא
בִּכְבוֹדוֹ וּבְעַצְמוֹ, שֶׁנֶּאֱמַר: וְעָבַרְתִּי בְאֶרֶץ מִצְרַיִם בַּלַּיְלָה
הַזֶּה, וְהִכֵּיתִי כָל בְּכוֹר בְּאֶרֶץ מִצְרַיִם מֵאָדָם וְעַד בְּהֵמָה, וּבְכָל
אֱלֹהֵי מִצְרַיִם אֶעֱשֶׂה שְׁפָטִים, אֲנִי יהוה.

וְעָבַרְתִּי בְאֶרֶץ מִצְרַיִם בַּלַּיְלָה הַזֶּה. אֲנִי וְלֹא מַלְאָךְ. וְהִכֵּיתִי כָל
בְּכוֹר בְּאֶרֶץ מִצְרַיִם. אֲנִי וְלֹא שָׂרָף. וּבְכָל אֱלֹהֵי מִצְרַיִם אֶעֱשֶׂה
שְׁפָטִים. אֲנִי וְלֹא הַשָּׁלִיחַ. אֲנִי יהוה. אֲנִי הוּא
וְלֹא אַחֵר.

And the Lord lifted us out of Egypt. Not by the hands of an Angel of Man, and not by the hands of an Angel Alight, and not by the hands of an Angel Redeeming, but rather it was done by the Holy One, Blessed is He; done by His Glorious Self - and by Himself, as it is said: And I will cross through the land of Egypt on this night, and I will strike every first-born in the land of Egypt from man to beast, and I - on all the gods of Egypt - will deliver judgment. I am the Lord!

And I will cross through the land of Egypt on this night.
I and not an Angel of Man.
And I will strike every first-born in the land of Egypt.
I and not an Angel Alight.
And I - on all the gods of Egypt - will deliver judgment.
I and not an Angel Redeeming.
I am the Lord! I am Him and no other.

065   064

The Haggadah is a collection of Biblical rituals and stories. The book includes a new translation with comments from some of the leading voices of Jewish literature. It has been edited by Jonathan Safran Foer and translated by Nathan Englander.

onlab

Berlin, Germany
http://onlab.ch

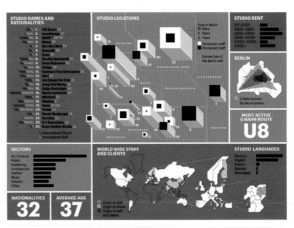

The Swiss graphic design agency onlab, founded in 2001 and based in Berlin, works on commissioned, collaborative as well as self-initiated design projects. The focus of the commissioned work lies in editorial design and visual communication projects. Some of the Onlab's projects have included the visual identity of the city of Tramelan, the redesign of the Italian architecture magazine *Domus* and the design and conception of the German contribution to the architecture Biennale in Venice 2008. Nicolas Bourquin is the founder and creative director. He was born in Switzerland in 1975 where he studied at the School of Design in Biel. Thibaud Tissot was born in La Chaux-de-Fonds in 1984 where he studied graphic design at the Design Academy. Niloufar Tajeri joined onlab as managing director. She was born in Tehran in 1980 and she was trained in architecture at the University of Karlsruhe, Germany.

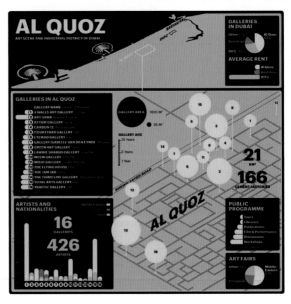

Design of two maps for the supplement of the German magazine *Wallpaper*, on the key graphic design studios in the city of Berlin and art galleries in the Al Quoz district of Dubai.

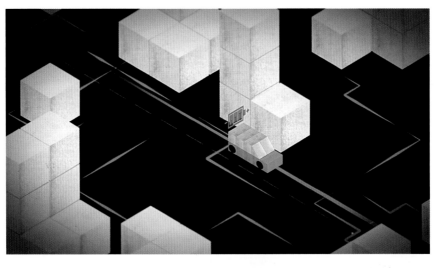

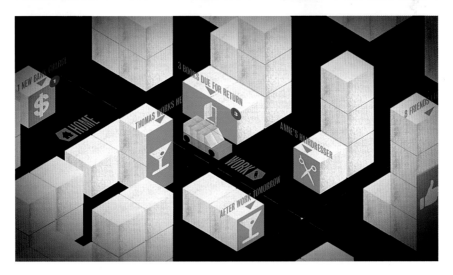

Clip for the car manufacturer Audi for the *Audi Urban Furniture Summit 2011*.

Since 2009, onlab has designed the posters for exhibitions in the Museum of Fine Arts in La Chaux-de-Fonds, Switzerland.

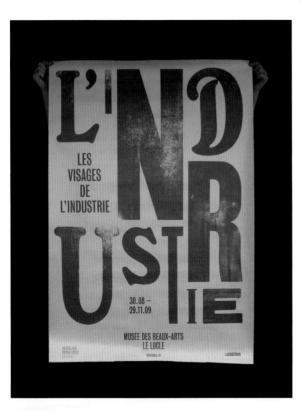

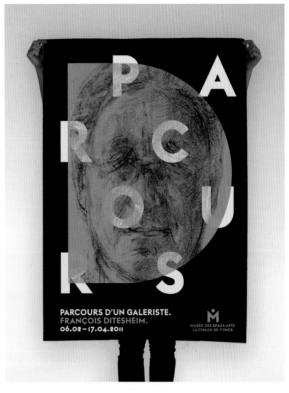

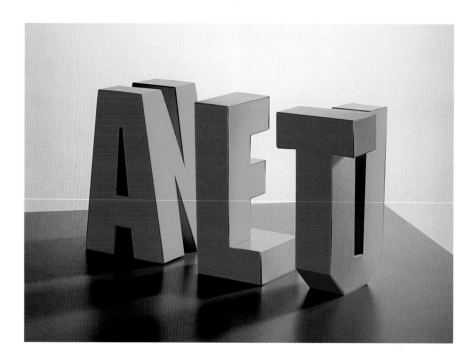

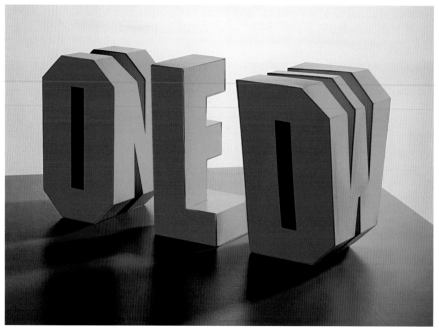

Editorial design handbook for the rehabilitation of old buildings, *Old & New, Alt und Neu* in German. Cover photos by Michel Bonvin.

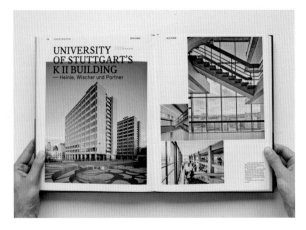

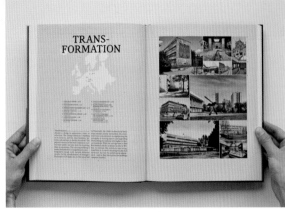

This book with 192 pages and 23 x 30 cm, published by Birkhäuser Verlag, details the main concepts to consider when dealing with the recovery of an old building.

Patswerk

The Hague, the Netherlands
www.patswerk.nl

Dutch-based graphic design & illustration agency Patswerk was founded in 2008 by longtime friends Ramon Avelino (1982), Rogier Mulder (1982) and Lex van Tol (1982). Our shared love for graffiti, drawing and graphic design is what binds us. Even though each of the Patswerk members has their own graphic style, we always try to combine our talent, and make each piece a team effort. In our work there is often a playful element. We like to use bright colors and hand drawn elements. We use many different techniques, both digital as well as manual, depending on the project we are working on.

Illustrations for CJP, a Dutch organization that promotes culture among teenagers. A character with many different features to choose from has been designed, so that students can design their own.

Personal illustration combining the style of each of the three designers of the studio.

Since 2008, the studio has designed the image of Doorzomer Festival, an annual event with music, art and drama that takes place in the Dutch city of Maassluis.

Design of two T-shirts for the *Artist Collection* by Freshcotton, an online urban clothing label.

Various graphic designs and educational material for children's workshops. In addition to a brochure that unfolds and becomes a poster, several briefcases were painted to use in one of the workshops.

1

1. *Good Hair day* is the title of this illustration, designed for the magazine *AMMO*.

2. Patswerk designed a lively and cheerful landscape that Grove, a small company in Oregon, laser engraved on bamboo for an iPhone cover.

2

Personal illustration with drawings of various animals made with the two-color silkscreen technique.

Design carried out as contribution to the exhibition *Don't Believe the Type*. Three ink screen printing.

Pierre Kurczewski/
Studio Lesbeauxjours

Saint-Nazaire, France
www.lesbeauxjours.fr

I work and live in France, in Saint-Nazaire, on the edge of the Atlantic Ocean, where the river Loire joins the sea. I work for what we call here the cultural sphere (music, theater, dance, arts). The name of my studio is lesbeauxjours and it's just me. Ironically, being a graphic designer, when I work on a project I almost never think of it as an image. Whether it is the creation of visual identity or a publishing project or the design of posters, it is the quest of the specific energy for the project that guides me. I do not think of the image as a representation but rather as energy and rhythm. The images presented in this book show this construction process.

Design of several posters for alternative cultural events: concerts, poetry and jazz events, etc.

Design of several posters for Farniente Festival 2011, an independent music festival.

One of the posters that was designed for independent concert hall La Nef.

Après *Hamlet* au VIP en 2009, et un mémorable *Richard III* au LiFE la saison dernière, **David Gauchard** et la **Cie L'unijambiste** ont concocté avec le fanal, le VIP et le soutien du LiFE, deux jours de musique, de théâtre et de cinéma.
David Gauchard est artiste associé au fanal 2009-2012.

CINÉ - CONCERT

L'AURORE « A SONG OF TWO HUMANS »

Friedrich Wilhelm Murnau | Olivier Mellano

JEUDI 15 DÉCEMBRE | 20h30

Depuis ses collaborations multiples aux côtés des grands noms de la scène française – Dominique A, Miossec, Yann Tiersen –, Olivier Mellano a gagné une place de musicien incontournable de la pop rock hexagonale. Mais il est aussi et surtout un auteur-compositeur-arrangeur surprenant. Il épouse ici les images sublimes de *L'Aurore* de Friedrich Wilhelm Murnau.
Séduit par une intrigante de la ville, un paysan tente de noyer son épouse lors d'une promenade sur le lac. Pris de remords, il ne parvient pas à commettre son crime. La jeune femme s'enfuit en ville. Elle est bientôt rejointe par son mari, désireux de se faire pardonner. Commence alors l'espoir du retour d'un bonheur que l'on croyait perdu à jamais.
La musique d'Olivier Mellano marque ici par sa fluidité. Sa lecture musicale de *L'Aurore* rehausse encore davantage la beauté du film, sans dénaturer la force poétique de ce chef-d'œuvre et souligne son incroyable modernité cinématographique.

Film muet de Friedrich Wilhelm Murnau (N&B -1927) avec George O'Brien, Janet Gaynor, Margaret Livingstone…
Accompagnement musical Olivier Mellano
Création en 2005 pour le Printemps de Septembre à Toulouse

CONCERT

ROBERT LE MAGNIFIQUE

JEUDI 15 DÉCEMBRE | 22h30 | au VIP

Accompagné de son Mpc, sa basse et de son talent de scratcheur, Robert le magnifique donne une dimension épique et bigarrée à ses expérimentations musicales. Il jongle avec les styles, puise dans la pop, le hip hop, la drum n'bass, et le trip hop, s'acoquine avec la musique contemporaine, pour mieux éclater les barrières, humaniser l'electro, et donner naissance à un registre riche et personnel.

14

LECTURE

PLEASE KILL ME, Part 1

L'histoire non censurée du punk racontée par ses acteurs

Legs Mc Neil & Gillian McCain | David Gauchard

VENDREDI 16 DÉCEMBRE | 19h30

Please Kill Me est le fruit (vénéneux) de centaines d'heures d'entretiens avec ceux qui ont animé l'un des mouvements culturels et musicaux les plus détonants de la fin du vingtième siècle : le punk-rock américain. Réalisé sous forme de montage nerveux, extrêmement vivant et souvent impitoyablement drôle ou tragique, ce livre nous offre une plongée incroyable dans la vie quotidienne pleine de bruit et de fureur, de drogues, de catastrophes, de sexe et de poésie (parfois) du Velvet Underground, des Stooges d'Iggy Pop, des New York Dolls et des Heartbreakers de Johnny Thunders, de Patti Smith, des Ramones, de Blondie et de dizaines d'autres. Aucune censure n'a cours, les amitiés indéfectibles côtoient les antipathies persistantes et les amours explosives…

mise en scène David Gauchard
avec Anne Buffet, Emmanuelle Hiron, Nicolas Maury, Vincent Mourlon, Nicolas Petisoff

CONCERT

OFTEN FALSE, PSYKICK LYRIKAH, FORTUNE et DJ RELOU KREW

VENDREDI 16 DÉCEMBRE | de 21h à 1h45 | au VIP

La soirée se prolonge au VIP où le voyage intérieur intense et intimiste de Laetitia Sheriff et d'Often False voisine avec le verbe acre et exigeant du rap electro et rock de Psykick Lyrikah. Le mix electro-rock déjanté et nerveux de DJ Relou Krew succède aux mélodies limpides et au groove sombre de Fortune.

Often False - **chant** Laetitia Sheriff **saxophone** François Jeanneau **guitare** Thomas Poli
Psykick Lyrikah - **voix** Arm **guitare** Olivier Mellano **basse, scratch, pads** Robert le Magnifique
Fortune - **chant, guitare, basse et clavier** Lionel Pierres **machines, clavier** Pierre Lucas **batterie, percussions** Hervé Loos
DJ Relou Krew - Nico-Icon - Sautenarcisse selectors

15

Design of poster and program of activities 2011 for LiFE, International Place of the Emergent Forms.

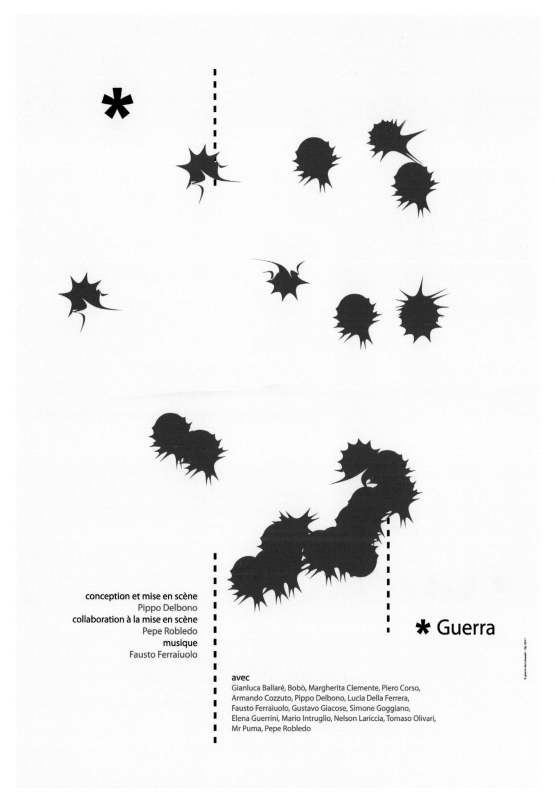

conception et mise en scène
Pippo Delbono
collaboration à la mise en scène
Pepe Robledo
musique
Fausto Ferraiuolo

* Guerra

avec
Gianluca Ballaré, Bobò, Margherita Clemente, Piero Corso,
Armando Cozzuto, Pippo Delbono, Lucia Della Ferrera,
Fausto Ferraiuolo, Gustavo Giacose, Simone Goggiano,
Elena Guerrini, Mario Intruglio, Nelson Lariccia, Tomaso Olivari,
Mr Puma, Pepe Robledo

Poster of the theatrical representation *War* by the Pippo Delbono company.

ProjectGRAPHICS

Pristina, Kosovo
www.projectgraphics.eu

ProjectGRAPHICS is a leading creative factory that brings together a group of young and inspiring talents in the field of brand identity, print and editorial design, packaging, interactive design and architecture. It nurtures a diverse interactive creativity since 2002, when it was founded by Agon Çeta, its lead designer, as a response to the overwhelming demands over his illustrious straight lined designs that marked his generation. The studio nourishes the concept of becoming one with the client, dousing the traditional perception of this bond and creating a new entity that strives to achieve perfection, both aesthetically and commercially. ProjectGRAPHICS artworks have been featured in many international design publications.

Bërthama is an advertising company. The corporate image design is based on the colors black and white as symbols of the unknown and what becomes known.

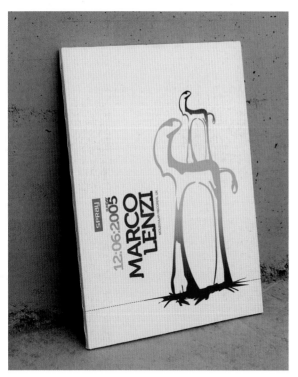

Design of several posters for a series of electronic music concerts in the city of Pristina.

Design of the visual identity and several posters for DAM, the International Festival of Young Musicians.

Design of several posters for plays represented at the National Theatre of Kosovo.

Design of the covers of several books for Multimedia,
Visual Arts Center.

Punkt

London, UK
www.punkt.com

I am Giles Dunn. I worked as a graphic designer since I graduated in 1989 from Central St. Martins. Over a period of five years I was part of what was then the Neville Brody Studio. After that stage I felt obliged to move to New York and founded my own agency: Punkt. Later, I created the fashion and accessories label Swami's, born of my love of surfing, design and craftsmanship. The label also satisfied my desire to work and create beyond the printed page. My job as a designer for the last twelve years has focused on commercial and cultural projects.

The project *Brand Tyranny* for *Graphis Magazine* reflects the saturation of brands.

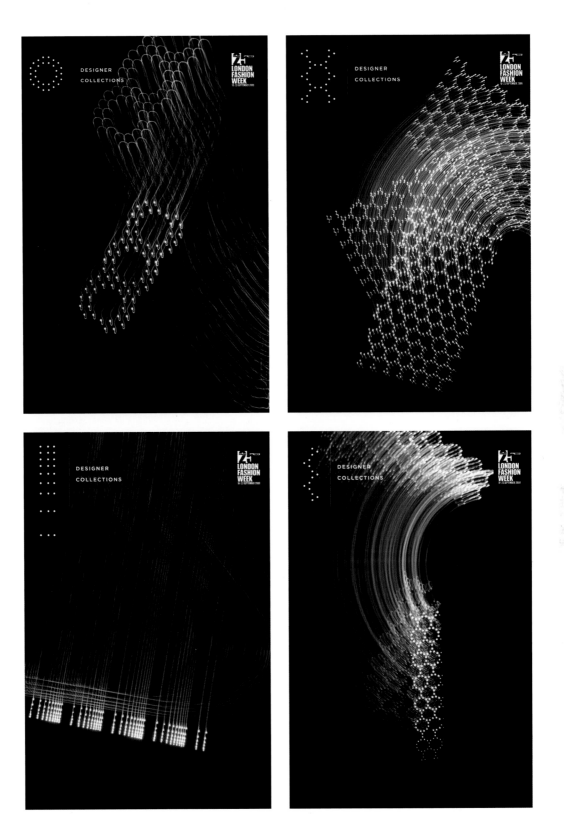

Design of a series of posters for the 25th
Anniversary of the London Fashion Week.

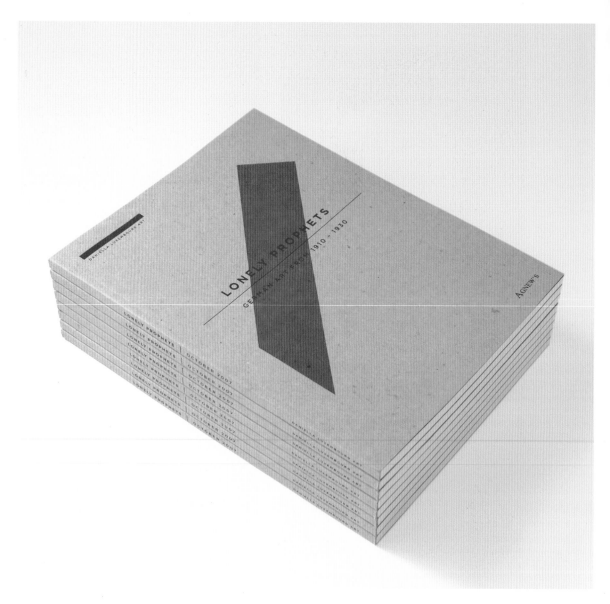

Commissioned by Daniella Luxembourg Art, Punkt
designed the catalog and the image of German
Expressionist art exhibition held in London *Lonely
Prophets. German Art from 1910 to 1930.*

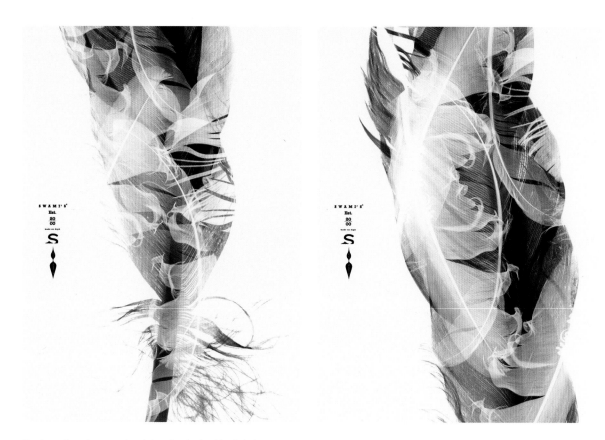

Design of posters and points of sale for the label
Swami's, created by the designer.

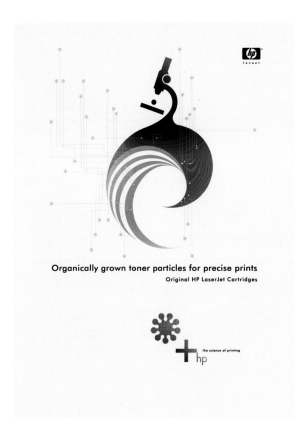

Organically grown toner particles for precise prints
Original HP LaserJet Cartridges

the science of printing
+hp

100 formulas to make one very pure hp ink
Original HP Ink

the science of printing
+hp

Billboard design for London Underground for the customer +Hp Supplies.

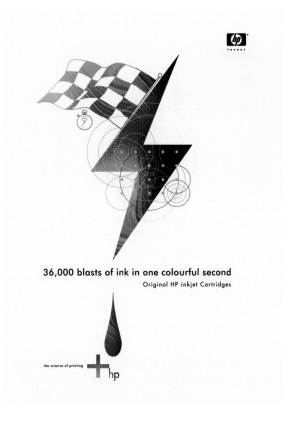

36,000 blasts of ink in one colourful second
Original HP inkjet Cartridges

the science of printing
+hp

The *Ryuichi Sakamoto's-Cinemage* project is CD packaging designed for
Sony Classic Design. The design is inspired by the emotional quality of
music by Sakamoto for the movies. Photography by Denise Milford.

Raffinerie

Zurich, Switzerland
www.raffinerie.com

Raffinerie AG für Gestaltung is a place where innovative ideas are transformed into high quality compositions. We offer the platform which makes the realization of creative potential accessible and secures the highly anticipated demand of compositive solutions. Raffinerie AG für Gestaltung was established in March 2000. The company is lead by Reto Ehrbar and Nenad Kovacic (both are partners and founders) plus Christian Haas. They employ a versatile team of designers and illustrators.

The gradation of color of the thermal imager was used for the design element of the catalog and the poster of the exhibition *Emergy Mountain*. The exhibition was created in collaboration with Holzer Kobler Architekturen.

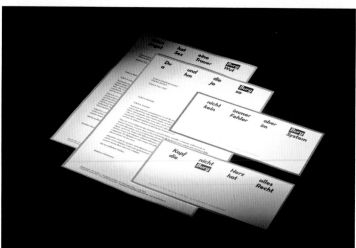

Die Burg is the most influential German theater in Europe. For its new corporate image the Neutra Face typeface was used, derived from a prototype of the architect Richard Neutra. The illustrations of the seasonal program are by Beni Bischof.

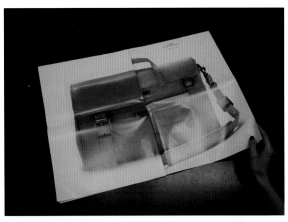

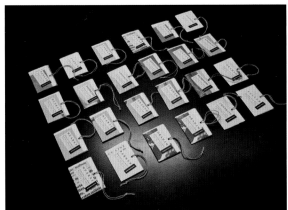

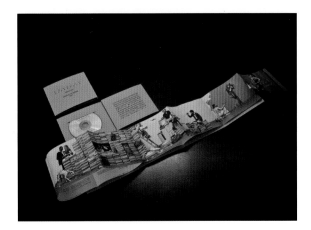

Promotional graphic elements for the new line of Freitag products, bag and briefcase company made with ad banner, created by brothers Markus and Daniel Freitag.

434

Poster design, invitation and exhibition program *Hund, Katz, Maus* in Zurich. Animal drawings extracted from paintings by artists from past decades were used.

Design of a guide to local shops and businesses in the popular district of
Langstrasse, Zurich.

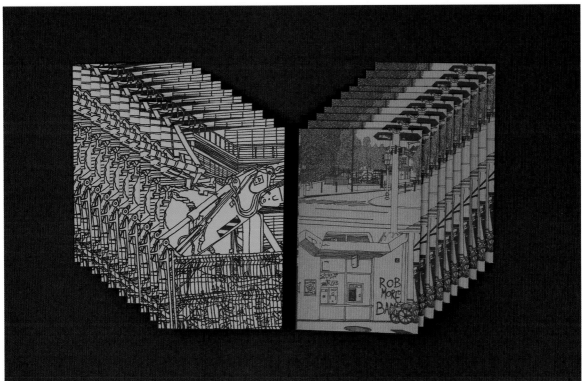

The typography and imagery are the basis of the graphic elements designed for Theaterhaus Gessnerallee. The semester program is the pinnacle of its communication material. The design allows for cost-effective production.

Ragnar Freyr

Reykjavik, Iceland
www.ragnarfreyr.com
www.createmake.com

I'm a graphic designer, web designer, illustrator, creator and maker from Reykjavík, Iceland. I'm married to the wonderful Ragnheiður Ösp and together we have Panda, the furbaby. I was born on the 26 July 1980 and I've been making websites, graphics and publications with varying levels of success since 1995. I officially started my own design studio in 2001. I believe in simplicity and the principles of minimalism in both life and design.

23.59

Breakbeat.is
í samstarfi
við Becks
og Jacobsen
kynnir:

All Nighter
á Jacobsen
föstudaginn
14. ágúst

Efri hæð
(house & grooves)
Ewok
Leópold
TZMP (Live)

Kjallari
(dnb & dubstep)
Breakbeat.is
fastasnúðar

Frítt inn

06.00

Design a poster for one of the events Breakbeat.is, a six-hour music session *Allnighter*.

Another of the posters designed for Breakbit.is. On this occasion it is a concert by the musician Hudson Mohawke.

1. Illustration of a window in Reykjavik for the magazine *GOOD 19: The Neighborhoods Issue*.

2. Logo designed for a secret musical project by Lazycomet called Mixme.

Poster for an event organized by Breakbeat.is, on this occasion a DJ session.

Series of posters designed for the EVE Fanfest 2001.

Richard B. Doubleday

Boston, MA, USA
http://richarddoubleday.com

I am an Assistant Professor at the College of Fine Arts, Boston University, and teach in the university's London Liberal Arts Program. My awards and honors include a Marion and Jasper Whiting Foundation Fellowship, and three Boston University Grants for Undergraduate Teaching and Scholarship. I have exhibited my poster designs at many international events and competitions. Recently, I led workshops at the Universidad Del Valle De Mexico, Hermosillo, Sonora, Mexico; and the Design College, Nanjing Arts Institute, China. My work has been published in several publications, including *The Poster: 1.000 Posters from Toulouse-Lautrec to Sagmeister* (Abrams, 2010) and *The Sourcebook of Contemporary Graphic Design* (HarperCollins, 2009).

Poster for workshop, conference and exhibition at Universidad del Valle de Mexico, in Hermosillo, Sonora.

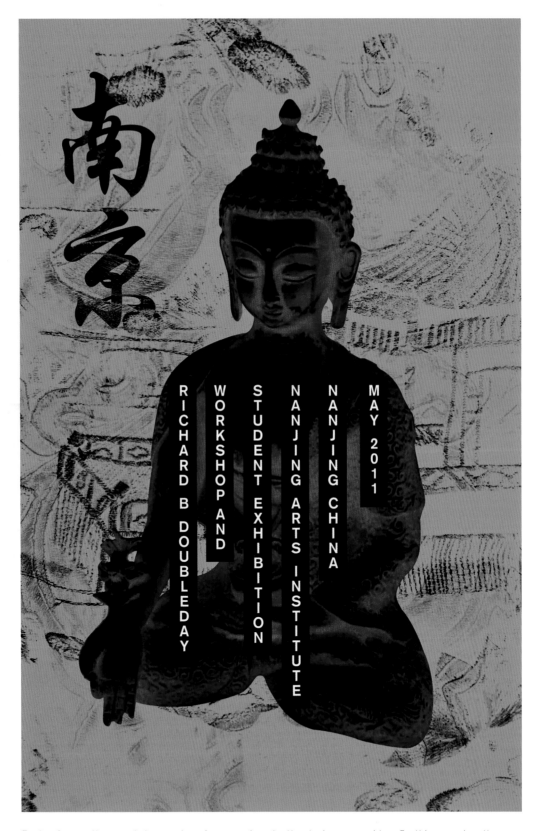

Poster for another workshop and conference given by the designer provides. On this occasion, the Nanjing Arts Institute, in Nanjing, China, in 2011.

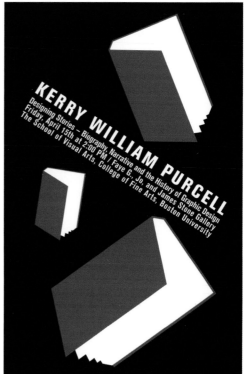

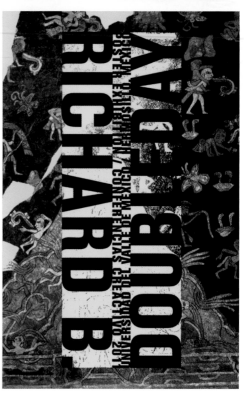

Local symbols are frequently used in the works by Richard B. Doubleday that exemplifies lectures and workshops.

RICHARD B. DOUBLEDAY EXHIBITION / CONFERENCIAS CREACTIVO 2011

UNIVERSIDAD DEL VALLE DE MEXICO HERMOSILLO, SONORA, MEXICO

Besides being a graphic designer specialized in the design of posters, Richard B. Doubleday is noted for his educational background and publications in which he has collaborated.

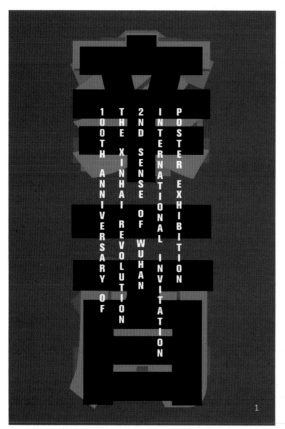

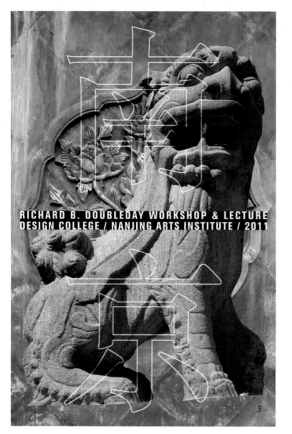

1-2. These posters were made to the *International Poster Exhibition* of the Art Museum in Wuhan, China, celebrating the centenary of the Xinhai Revolution.

3. Another piece of work from the series of posters for the Nanjing Arts Institute in 2011 to mark the workshop given by the designer.

In the Nanjing school workshop, students chose a personal theme or cultural and artistic events from the last decade. The aim was to combine multiple data and create a representation of a single visual support.

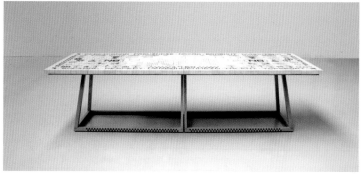

Roel Vaessen

'S-Hertogenbosch, the Netherlands
www.roelvaessen.nl

I'm a Dutch Graphic Designer. I like
to collaborate with other designers
(Marloes de Laat, Studio Parade).
I think it's interesting to combine
graphic design with spatial design.
Together with Eric Sloot and Paulien
Berendsen I have developed and designed Ixxi (www.ixxi.nu), a new interior product/connecting system,
which lets you design your own wallpaper in any size you want. I also like
to design printwork , like books, publications and corporate identities.

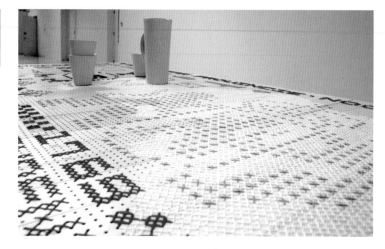

This table, gift for the Queen's Commissioner for the province of Brabant,
is used in the commissioner's meetings and symbolizes the values of the
Brabant region: industry, commerce, innovation and design.

Design awards for Dutch Design Awards 2008 in collaboration with
Studio Parade (www.studioparade.nl).

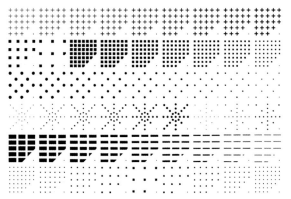

Design of the frame for shelf modules for the Eindhoven Design Academy, carried out for Studio Parade.

Program of activities with the theme *Reset the City*, organized by the Bosch Architecture Initiative.

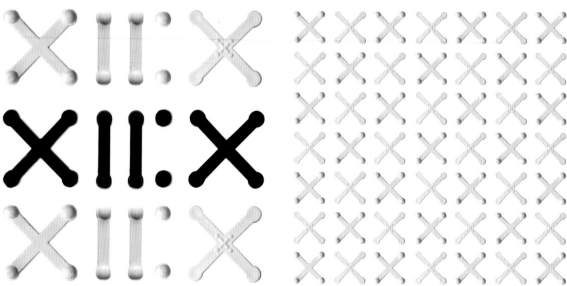

IXXI is a system to join decorative panels developed
by Roel Vaessen. The pieces can create wall panels of
varying sizes with customized images.

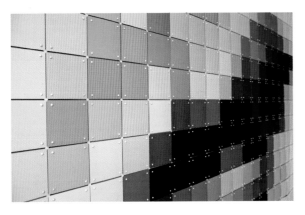

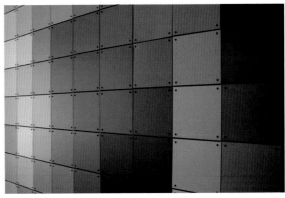

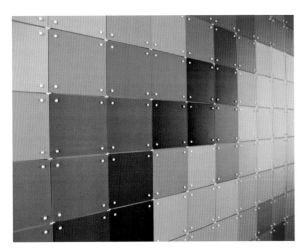

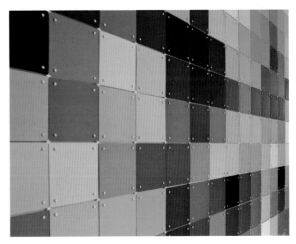

Thanks to IXXI different decorations can be created. The colored panels, strategically placed, form a pixilated image, such as the reproduction of the painting *The girl with a Pearl*.

Sam Wiehl/Burn Everything

Liverpool, UK
www.burneverything.co.uk

I am a designer working in graphics, illustration, interior & event design and moving image. I have been co-running Burneverything (which recently closed its doors) for the last 10 years and now I work between Liverpool and New York. I spend slightly too long on projects but strangely don't mind. Clients I have worked with include companies such as Google, Tate, Volvo, Sony and the Radisson Hotel Group. The selection of works I have included here are my recent music-related projects.

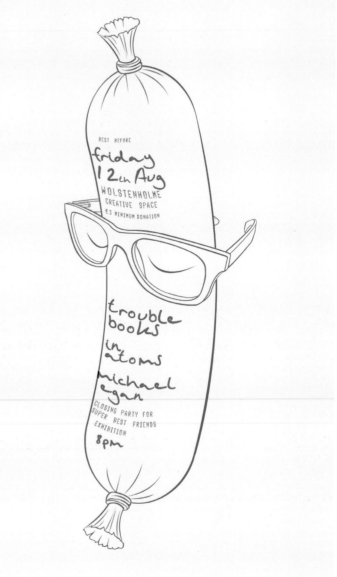

Behind The Wall of Sleep

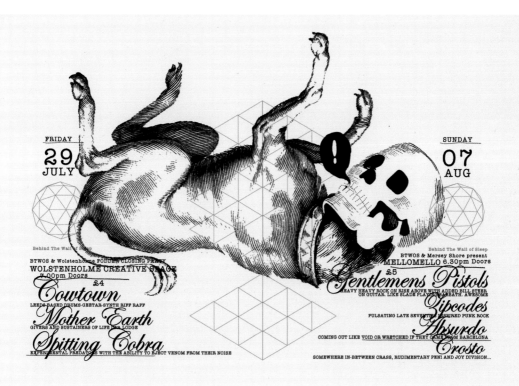

FRIDAY
29
JULY

SUNDAY
07
AUG

Behind The Wall of Sleep

BTWOS & Wolstenholme FODDER CLOSING PARTY
WOLSTENHOLME CREATIVE SPACE
7.00pm Doors
£4

Cowtown
LEEDS-BASED DRUMS-GEETAR-SYNTH RIFF RAFF

Mother Earth
GIVERS AND SUSTAINERS OF LIFE IN A LODGE

Spitting Cobra
EXPERIMENTAL PREDATORS WITH THE ABILITY TO EJECT VENOM FROM THEIR NOISE

Behind The Wall of Sleep

BTWOS & Mersey Shore present
MELLOMELLO 6.30pm Doors
£5

Gentlemens Pistols
HEAVY HEAVY ROCK ON RISE ABOVE WITH ADDED BILL STEER
ON GUITAR. LIKE SLADE PLAYING SABBATH. AWESOME

Zipcodes
PULSATING LATE SEVENTIES INSPIRED PUNK ROCK

Absurdo
COMING OUT LIKE VOID OR WRETCHED IF THEY CAME FROM BARCELONA

Crosto
SOMEWHERE IN-BETWEEN CRASS, RUDIMENTARY PENI AND JOY DIVISION...

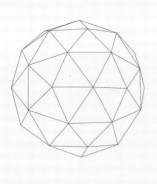

Behind The Wall Of Sleep

Behind The Wall Of Sleep

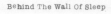

Design of identity and posters, some of them screenprinted, for the art collection Behind the Wall of Sleep.

457

Corporate identity and marketing activities for the audiovisual art group The Hive Collective. It includes interactive projects that were part of the Digital Art Festival Futureverything, held in Manchester.

PHILIP JECK works with old records and record players salvaged from junk
shops, turning them to his own purposes. He really does play them as musical
instruments, creating an intensely personal language that evolves with each
added part of a record.
Philip Jeck makes genuinely moving and transfixing music,
where we hear the art not the gimmick.

HIVESESSIONS

Thur 24th March / from 8pm free

PHILIP JECK

We're pleased to announce the first of our regular
HIVEsessions at Leaf starting on Thur 24 March.
Free, themed and dj led, they offer a refreshing take on city centre
listening from the outer limits. Quality guests and the occasional
live act from across the electronic music spectrum join the HIVE
residents and visual artists, all for free.

LEAF - Bold Street Liverpool

www.thehivecollective.co.uk

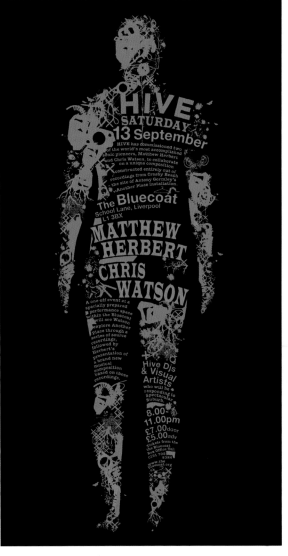

Design of posters for various events organized by the music and visual arts groups The Hive Collective. In this particular case, a series of shows in which the invited artists reinterpret the notions of physical space.

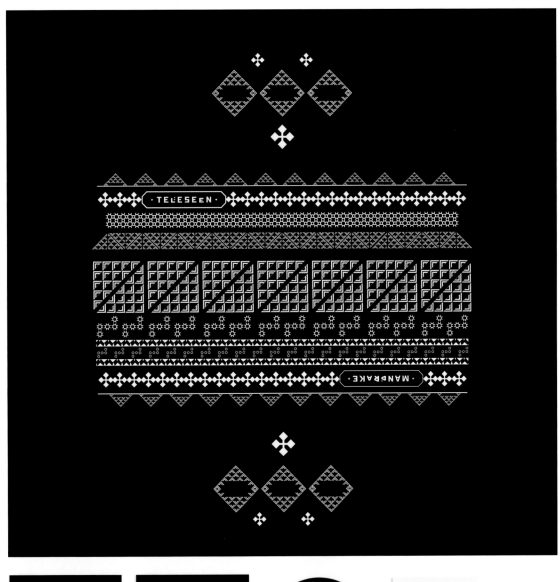

Packaging design for the electronic artist Teleseen living in New York. The design includes a postcard numbered by hand.

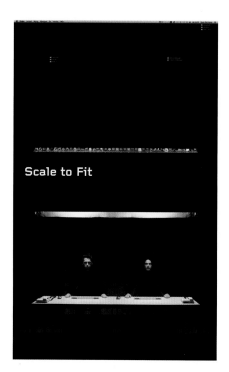

Scale to Fit

Rotterdam, the Netherlands
www.scaletofit.com

We're a visual communication bureau based in Rotterdam, the Netherlands. We both, Dennis and Hans, grew up in the south of Holland. We met at high school, where we organized school parties at clubs, did graffiti and skateboarded for most of the time. After moving to the big cities for art school we both worked at some agencies in Holland. In spite of our jobs, we kept working together at the weekends and late at night. Until, we got some major assignments and together we formed Scale to Fit. After a few years of hard work and building our network, we're doing lot's of work in music, festivals and we have some serious clients. Our next step will be to help our clients to be more conscious about their business goals and values. And to translate this through design (thinking) into communication items and services off and online.

Circusstad Festival is a cultural festival that for five days fills the streets of the city of Rotterdam with musical shows. Posters, website and logo were designed for the festival.

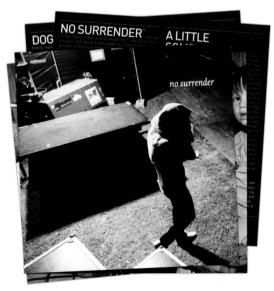

Kane is a popular Dutch rock band. Scale to Fit had already designed some of their album covers. *No Surrender* is the latest.

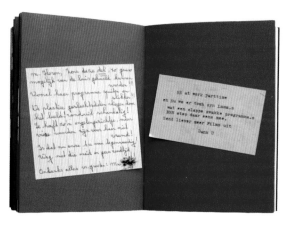

BNN is a radio station with a loyal and young following. This book can
be customized, allowing each reader to add personal items.

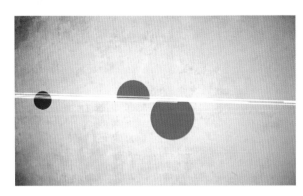

CD and music video design for singer Chris LeMay.

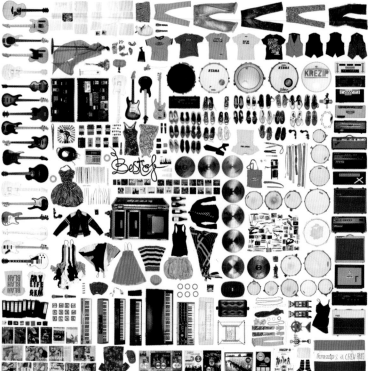

For the cover of the Krezip compilation album, objects and memorabilia of its ten year career are used such as guitars, CDs, emails from fans, clothing etc.

Krezip is a successful Dutch band with a history of more than ten years. The image of its compilation album conveys vitality and energy.

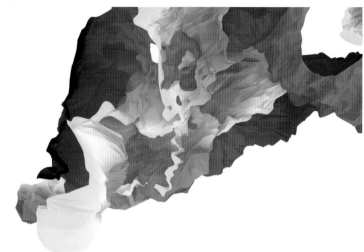

SEA Design

London, UK
www.seadesign.co.uk

I studied Graphic Design at New-
castle Polytechnic, and after graduating in 1992 I began my career at
Roundel Design Group. Together with
John Simpson I founded the multidisciplinary design consultancy SEA
in 1997. My work and experience has
touched many disciplines; from corporate identity and art direction to
print, packaging, information design
and moving image. I have worked with
a range of public and private sector
clients including Jamie Oliver, Adidas/
Porsche, EMI, Global Cool, The Barbi-
can, Selfridges, Boots, and Burberry.
My work has been widely published
and has received recognition in a
number of national and international
design awards.

Art direction and design of a campaign for the digital promotion of paper
for GF Smith.

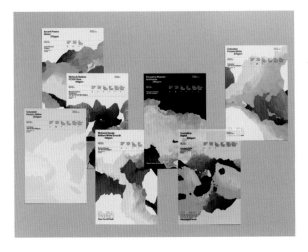

The automatic generation process, mixed with the code and a default color palette, created 10,000 unique digital prints.

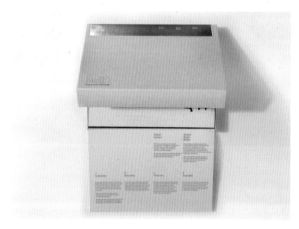

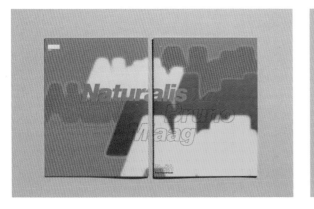

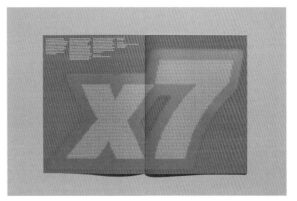

So let's talk about Aktiv, Dalton Maag's new Helvetica killer. Can you design a typeface in opposition to something? Is that what you set out to do or were you just trying to create as good a grotesk as you could for general use? Clearly, because we are competing against Univers, Akzidenz and Helvetica there are a lot of close similarities. The x height is fractionally higher than Helvetica but the rounds have a little bit of squareness about them that Helvetica's don't have. The differences are really subtle but give it just that bit of personality. It was two-pronged really. One was the fact that we were looking at our font library and felt that we were missing a pure grotesk in a Univers style, purely as a commercial entity. It has been at the back of our minds to do this for the last three or four years now. We wanted to have a grotesk font positioned somewhere between Helvetica and Univers – not as icy cold as Univers but devoid of all the quirks of Helvetica. To have a font that is beautifully crafted, spaced well, with not a chink in a curve or anything – perfectly drawn but hopefully with a bit of personality. We wanted to create something that could be used in a corporate environment but has that bit of warmth that Univers doesn't have.

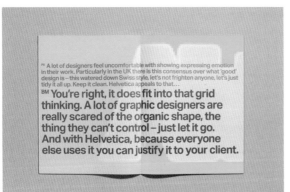

A lot of designers feel uncomfortable with showing expressing emotion in their work. Particularly in the UK there is this consensus over what 'good' design is – this watered down Swiss style, let's not frighten anyone, let's just tidy it all up. Keep it clean. Helvetica appeals to that…

You're right, it does fit into that grid thinking. A lot of graphic designers are really scared of the organic shape, the thing they can't control – just let it go. And with Helvetica, because everyone else uses it you can justify it to your client.

How can you use it wrongly?

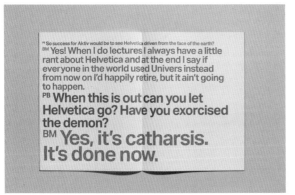

So success for Aktiv would be to see Helvetica driven from the face of the earth?

Yes! When I do lectures I always have a little rant about Helvetica and at the end I say if everyone in the world used Univers instead from now on I'd happily retire, but it ain't going to happen.

When this is out can you let Helvetica go? Have you exorcised the demon?

Yes, it's catharsis. It's done now.

Corporate identity, strategic positioning and art direction for the independent commercial paper company GF Smith.

471

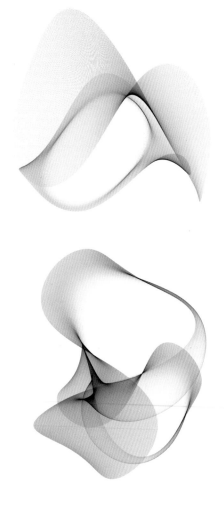

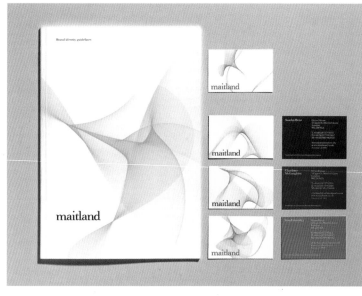

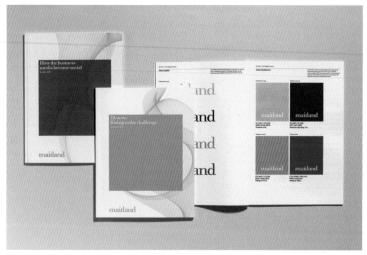

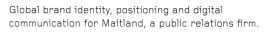

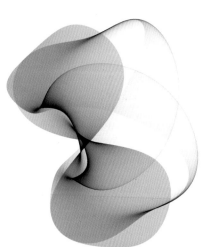

Global brand identity, positioning and digital communication for Maitland, a public relations firm.

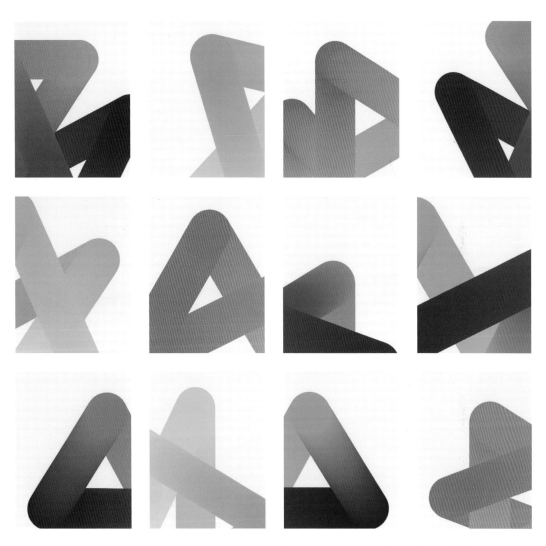

Design of web and style guide for APBL
architectural studio, based in London and
Winchester.

Design of identity and website for the K2 Silkscreen print studio.

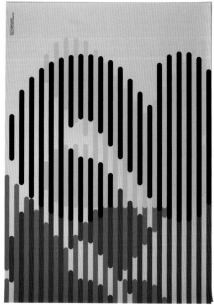

K2 Screen
Unit B5/16—16A Bal
info@K2screen.
Telephone 020

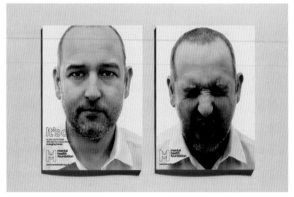

Design of strategic vision, corporate identity and visual communication for the Mental Health Foundation UK.

Strategic positioning of brand and identity design of Sansaw, a rural estate located in Shropshire. This estate blends traditional life, close to nature with the modern world.

Serial Cut

Madrid, Spain
www.serialcut.com

My name is Sergio del Puerto, I'm the
founder and creative director of my
studio, Serial Cut™, which I founded
in 1999. A lot of time has passed and
many things too... I studied Visual
Communication and I started to work
in a lifestyle magazine called *Vanidad*. I
also illustrated for the Spanish newspaper *El País*. After that I started to
do freelance work and sought out my
own clients including many studios
and agencies. Years later, I decided
to open my studio and dedicate myself
full time to my business. What I have
always had clear is that good work
can always be improved. Serial Cut™
has grown from being a one person
studio, it now employs four people
and has other external contributors,
working on international projects with
clients such Nike, Zune, MTV, Chan-
nel4, Toyota, Rolling Stone, Diesel...
We are still a small studio, but with
some big clients.

Promotional images by the studio with elements that refer to typical
Spanish food. Photos by Paloma Rincón.

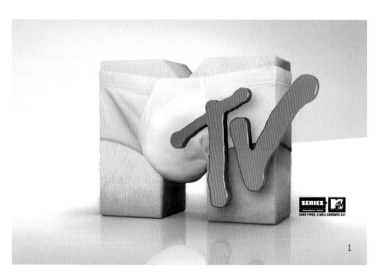

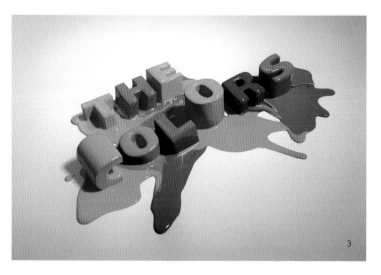

1. Promotional image for the MTV teen comedy *Hard Times*.

2. Promotional image by the studio was inspired by a painting from the 70's and in collaboration with Jimmy Andersson.

3. Promotional image for the Jotun paint brand. The letters are covered with real paint. Photography by Paloma Rincón.

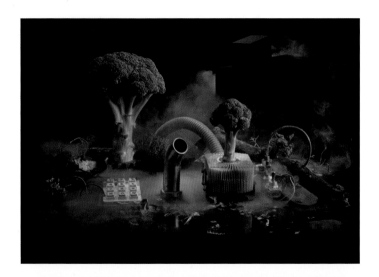

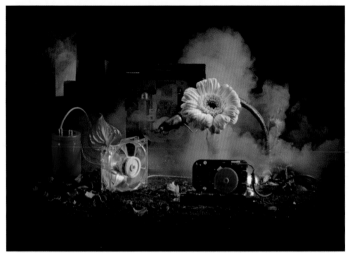

This project, entitled *Plant Station* and with the collaboration of
Kristian Touborg is a commissioning for Studio Output London by
Sony Playstation. The images are used to customize the PS3 and PSP.
Photography by Paloma Rincón.

1. Still life of real objects and fonts in blocks of gelatin. Collaboration with Mr. Oso® and designer Kristian Touborg. Photography by Paloma Rincón.

2. Image to promote the cuisine of Singapore, commissioned by Yoursingapur.com.

Smel

Amsterdam, the Netherlands
www.smel.net

Smel, founded in 2001 by Edgar Smaling and Carlo Elias, consists of a dynamic team of dedicated, multidisciplinary creative people. We design strategic corporate identities, magazines, books, websites... illustrious design concepts that subtly unite quality and imagination. We work for a variety of clients covering public services, fashion, design, art and architecture. Smel is an open ideas company renowned for its high-end graphic design. Our attitude to design is hybrid. Thanks to our nationwide and international network of dedicated communications and media professionals, big projects become small and small ones grow bigger.

Made of Japan is a bilingual Japanese-English publication, designed by Smel and by the creative team of the magazine *Zoo*, held to celebrate the 60th anniversary of the sneakers brand Onitsuka Tiger.

ZOO MAGAZINE

ZOO GERMANY–2011 NO.30
Angela Lindvall by Philip Gay

GERMANY € 7.50
Europe € 8.00
United Kingdom £ 6.99
USA US$ 15.00
Japan ¥ 1700.00
Australia AU$ 12.95
Canada CAN$ 15.00

top *Lanvin* earrings *Dary's*

**BAMBOU / DIANA DONDOE
SUBODH GUPTA / DREE HEMINGWAY
MICHAEL KUNZE / JT LEROY
ANGELA LINDVALL / DANNY TREJO
A.F. VANDEVORST AND MORE...**

Since 2007, Smel has been responsible for the design and art direction of the fashion and trend magazine *Zoo* in collaboration with Sandor Lubbe.

484

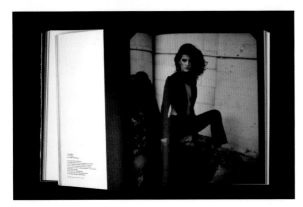

Design of corporate image and brand for the fashion label Just BS. Invitations to fashion shows where the collections were presented were designed.

Design of the limited edition box-book *Dimensions of Ambiguity*, which reproduces the work of Terry Rodgers. The box contains a book, an imprint of the artist's work and a piece of lingerie by Marlies Dekkers.

Staynice

Breda, the Netherlands
www.staynice.nl

We are two brothers, Rob and Barry van Dijck, the leaders of design agency Staynice. In 2007, we started our company, after graduating from AKV St.Joost, academy of fine arts in Breda. Our characteristic work drew a lot of attention at the academy. We were both nominated for the St.Joost penning, an award to the most promising student. Our motive is to leave something personal behind, something which lasts. We try to achieve a contemporary style for our assignments and our personal work; we try to translate digital aesthetics to the physical world. Typography forms part of most of our work as an important starting point. We have created several books and magazines, stationeries, posters, illustrations, websites, animations and so on. At the beginning of 2010 our work was exhibited at the Graphic Design Museum in Breda. Our roots lie in the graffiti and street-art movement.

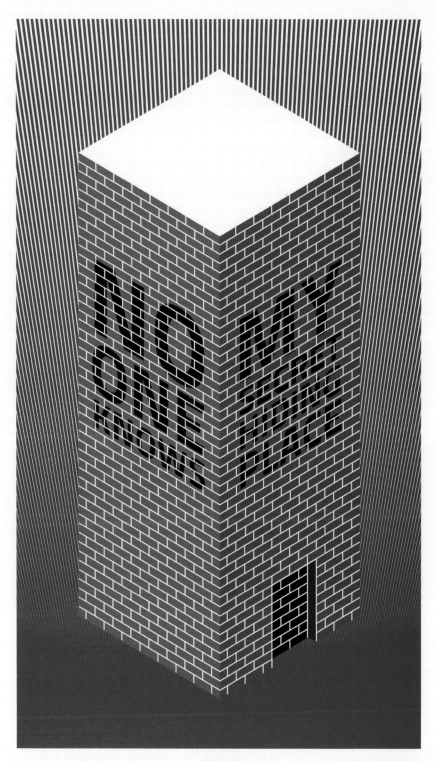

STAYNICE

The installation *No One Knows My Secret Hiding Place* was made for the Night of Culture Festival in Breda. Depending on how the light impinges on the poster, you can read the text on one area or another of the poster. The rest of the words are hidden.

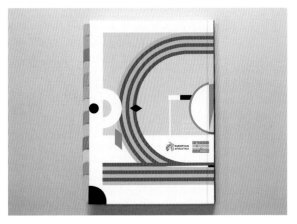

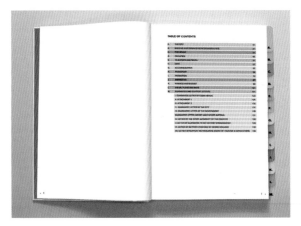
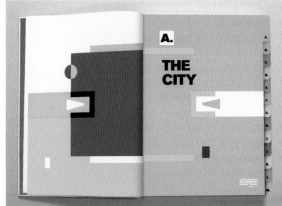

Design and layout of the publication *EK Bidbook*, for
TEAM Amsterdam, to mark the celebration of the
European Athletics Championships 2016.

Personal project. Christmas greetings from the Staynice studio for the 2011 holidays.

Design of the poster for the documentary *Het Geloof Van De Vliegende Vogels*, by the independent filmmaker Sabine König for Zuidenwind Filmproductions.

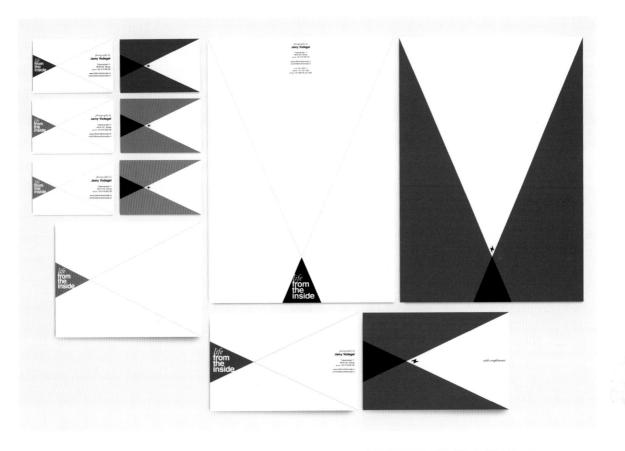

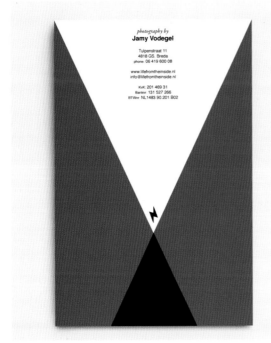

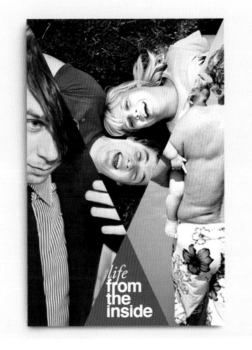

Corporate identity and stationery for the photography studio Life from the Inside.

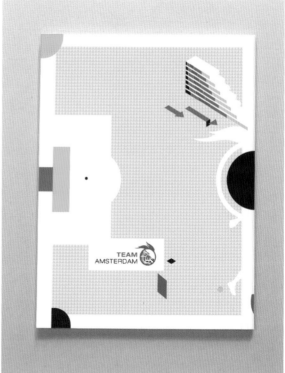

Brochure design and creation of illustrations for TEAM Amsterdam, through the agency Biqini Amsterdam.

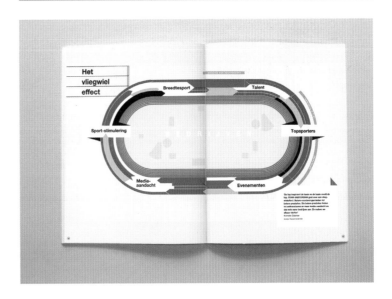

Stiletto NYC

Milan, Italy
www.stilettonyc.com

Stiletto NYC is a design studio based in Milan & New York, that specializes in art direction & design for print and video. It was co-founded in NYC in 2000 by Stefanie Barth and Julie Hirschfeld. Stiletto has worked with such clients as Conde Nast, *Double magazine*, *Good Magazine*, HBO, HKM films, Levis, Mercedes Benz, MTV, Nickelodeon, Nike, the nonprofit organization Not on Our Watch (co-founded by George Clooney), *New York Magazine*, *The New York Times*, Reebok, Sundance Channel, Andrea Tognon Architecture as well as smaller boutiques, artists and galleries in the US and Europe. Stiletto has won various industry awards and their work has been featured in publications around the world. Since 2010, Stiletto and Paris-based art director Carina Frey have been collaborating on art directing and designing *Double magazine* and for various fashion brands.

Levi's ad, summer 2011. Art direction by Carina Frey and photography by Boo George.

Art direction and design for the German glass company Owl. It includes the corporate identity, logo, website, brochures and stationery. Photography by Kira Bunse.

Art direction and design of the Parisian *Double Magazine*, in collaboration with Carina
Frey in the art direction and Fabrice Paineau in the edition.

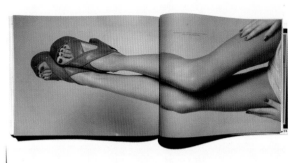

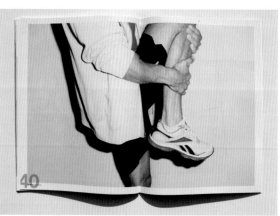

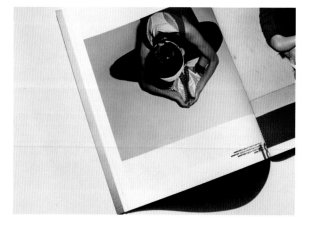

Design of catalogs for Reebok, summer 2011 season for men and women. Photography by Magnus Unnar.

Design and art direction for classic Reebok products.

Studio Job

Antwerp, Belgium
www.studiojob.be

Job Smeets and Nynke Tynagel graduated from the Eindhoven Design Academy, they founded Studio Job in 2000 and currently have offices in Belgium and Holland. They redefine the decorative arts from a contemporary point of view and blend the traditional with the modern and the organic with the artificial. They have worked with brands such as Bulgari, Swarovski, Bisazza, Venini, Royal Tichelaar Makkum and Moooi and have also exhibited in New York, Tokyo, Los Angeles, Paris, London, Milan, Geneva, Miami and Basel. In late 2009, they opened their own gallery for exhibitions of contemporary art and design in Antwerp. In 2010, the Rizzoli publishing house published *The Book of Job*, a collection of his work.

Although this studio is specialized in industrial design, the monograph project has allowed them to make a foray into the field of graphic design with remarkable success.

The editorial design of the monograph *The Book of Job* and its luxurious binding is reminiscent of the old Bibles. This resource has been used taking advantage of the fact that the studio's name can make use of this play on words.

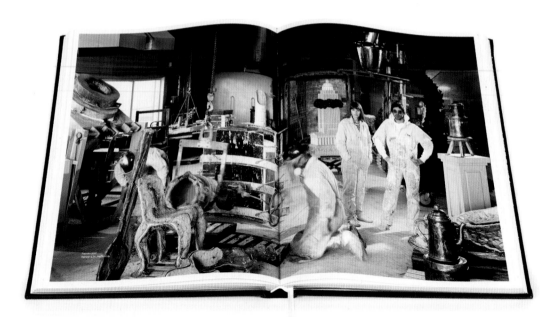

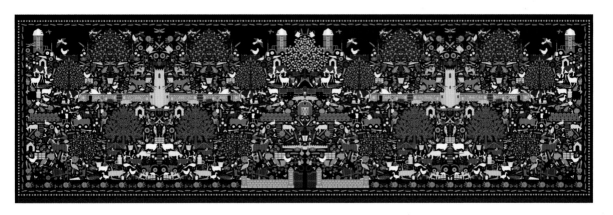

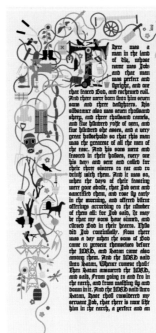

The combination of a medieval font with photographs taken expressly for the book generates a mixture of transgressive styles, in keeping with the other designs by Job Smeets and Nynke Tynagel.

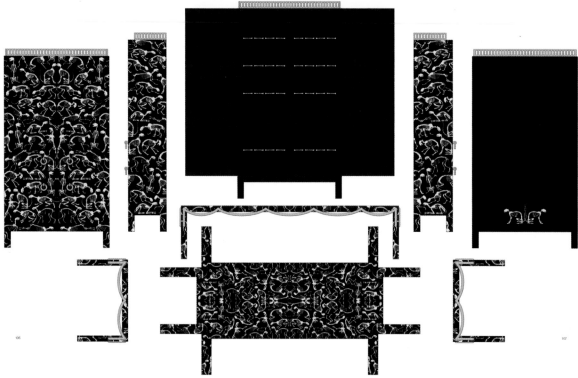

The staging of the works by Studio Job follows a theatrical aesthetic that defines the design of many of its works.

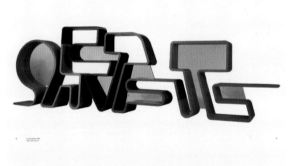

Studio Job's work published in this volume helps us to find out more about the creative process and sources of inspiration of these young designers.

Studio Jona

Amsterdam, the Netherlands
www.studiojona.nl

In 2001, I started Studio Jona to work for cultural and commercial clients. My main goal is to surprise a target group with simple, curious work that has a relevant message. One of my influences is the Belgian painter Magritte, he always comes back to me, just like the music of The Beatles. They are amazing. The directness and simplicity of their work has a huge impact on me. As a freelance designer and art director I've developed a wide range of works such as corporate identities, website design and execution, advertising, animations, brochures, folders and flyers, etc.

The posters for the annual Uitmarkt festival in Amsterdam invites spectators to come into contact with culture.

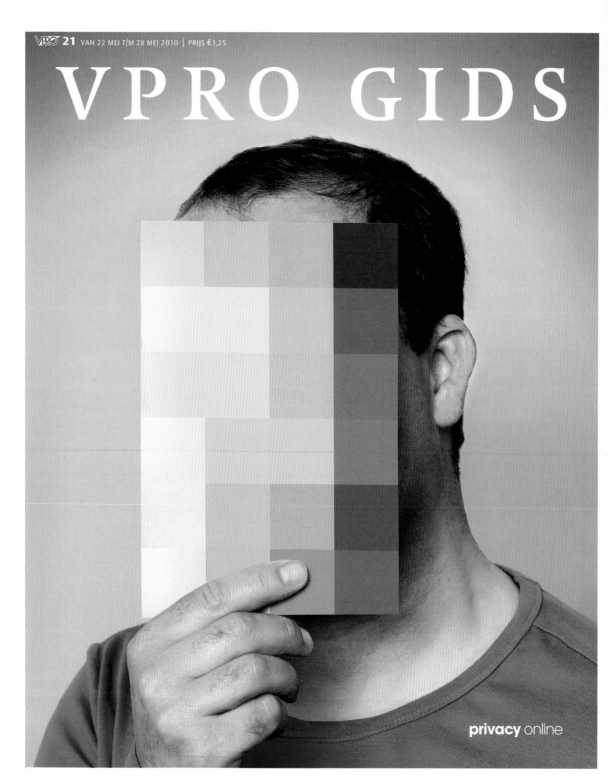

The cover of the TV Guide VPRO reflects on how to manage your values of digital life and how social networks affect our identity. This cover was winner in 2010 of the Lamp ADCN prize, the prestigious Dutch design awards.

In his show *Incriminating Evidence*, the comedian Jochen Otten condemns and defends himself. How to visualize the weight of your conscience? Studio Jona represents it using a huge heavy head to carry around.

The show by the comedian Klaas is about how quickly the years pass by. Klaas feels outdated, hence the aesthetics of the poster, which looks like a magazine ad from the 70s.

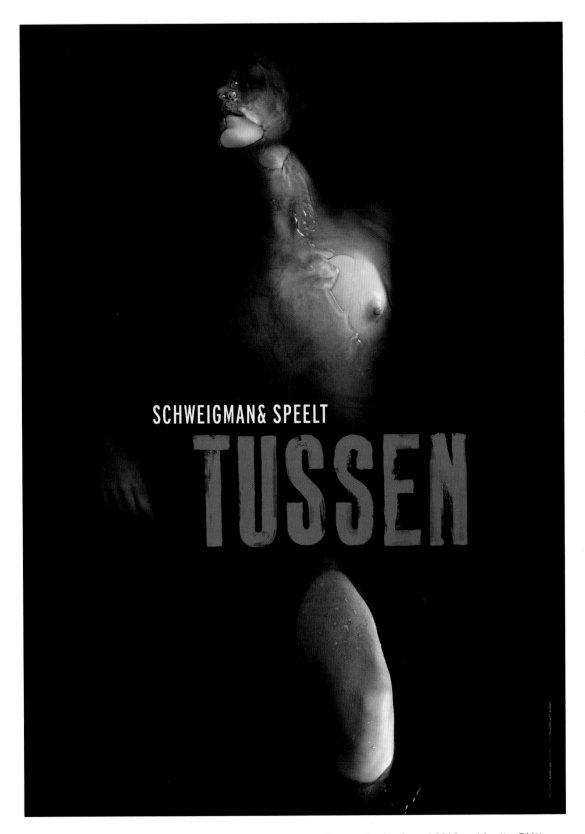

SCHWEIGMAN& SPEELT

TUSSEN

This poster for a play was nominated for best graphic design Theatre Poster Award 2010 and for the PANL Award for Best Dutch Photography.

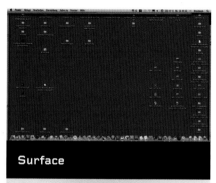

Surface

Frankfurt, Germany
www.surface.de

For over ten years, Surface has worked almost solely on themes of contemporary and performing arts, architecture, music and exhibition contexts. The conception design approach is dependent on the content of the inquiries and subjects are developed accordingly, in order to avoid style arbitrariness. Its client portfolio includes nationally and internationally renowned cultural institutions and companies, such as the Serpentine Gallery, London, Hugo Boss, Sternberg Press, Jewish Museum Berlin, DuMont Press, Siemens Art Program, Documenta, Jewish Museum, German Architectural Museum, Staedel Art School Frankfurt and Museum of Modern Art Frankfurt. Surface employs ten professional designers in Frankfurt and Berlin. The management is lead by Markus Weisbeck, who founded the studio in 1997.

Promotion of the artist Liam Gillick for the German pavilion at the 2009 Venice Biennale.

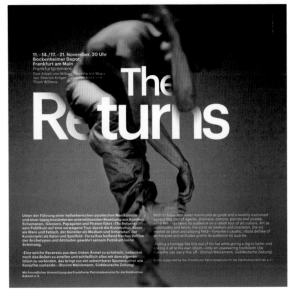

Image of 2011/2012 season for the dance group The Forsythe Company. Photography by Dominik Mentzer.

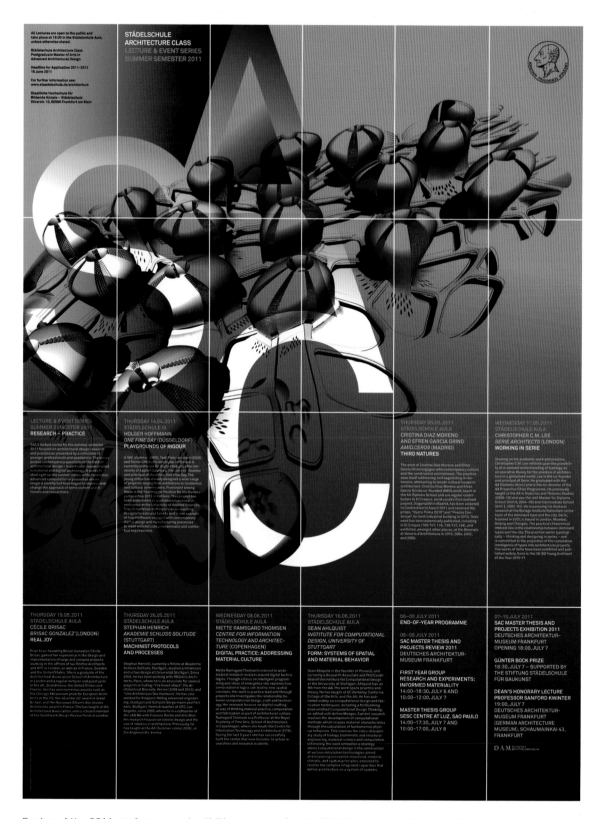

**STÄDELSCHULE
ARCHITECTURE CLASS
LECTURE & EVENT SERIES
SUMMER SEMESTER 2011**

**LECTURE & EVENT SERIES
SUMMER SEMESTER 2011
STÄDELSCHULE**
RESEARCH – PRACTICE

SAC's lecture series for the summer semester 2011 focuses on architectural design research and practice as presented by a collection of younger professionals and academics. The series probes contemporary questions in the field of architectural design – in particular issues related to material and digital technology. It seeks to shed light on the current status in the field when advanced computational processes are no longer a novelty but have begun to impress and change the approach of some current practitioners and researchers.

**THURSDAY 14.04.2011
STÄDELSCHULE IB
HOLGER HOFFMANN**
ONE FINE DAY (DÜSSELDORF)
PLAYGROUNDS OF RIGOUR

A SAC alumnus (2005), Test Preis recipient (2008) and former UNStudio employee, Hoffmann is currently professor for digital design at the University of Applied Sciences, Trier, and co-founder and principal of the office, One Fine Day. The young office has already designed a wide range of projects ranging from exhibitions to residential and cultural commissions. Prominent among these is the free-lounge Pavilion for the Bundesgartenschau 2011 in Koblenz. This project has been undertaken as a collaborative research endeavour at the University of Applied Sciences, Trier. It combines Hoffmann's wide-reaching design interests and talents and is one example of how Hoffmann engages with contemporary digital design and manufacturing processes to meet with delicate programmatic and contextual requirements.

**THURSDAY 05.05.2011
STÄDELSCHULE AULA
CRISTINA DIAZ MORENO
AND EFREN GARCIA GRIND**
AMID.CERO9 (MADRID)
THIRD NATURES

The work of Cristina Diaz Moreno and Efren Garcia Grind engages with contemporary culture and the constructed environment. This practice sees itself addressing and negotiating in-between, attempting to locate cultural issues in architecture. Cristina Diaz Moreno and Efren Garcia Grinda co-founded AMID.cero9, teach in the AA Diploma School and are regular contributors to El Croquis. amid.cero9's first realized project, Dragon#10 in Madrid, has been selected to ContractWorld Award 2011 and received the prizes, "Opera Prima 2010" and "Premio Construye", for best industrial building in 2010. Their work has been extensively published, including in El Croquis (106/107, 118, 139/133, 145), and exhibited, amongst other places, at the Biennale di Venezia d'Architettura in 2010, 2006, 2002, and 2000.

**WEDNESDAY 11.05.2011
STÄDELSCHULE AULA
CHRISTOPHER C.M. LEE**
SERIE ARCHITECTS (LONDON)
WORKING IN SERIE

Drawing on his academic work and practice, Christopher C.M. Lee reflects upon the possibility of a renewed understanding of typology as an operative theory for the practice of architecture in a globalised world. Lee is the co-founder and principal of Serie. He graduated with the AA Diploma (Hons) and is the co-director of the AA Projective Cities Programme. He previously taught at the AA in Histories and Theories Studies (2009–10) and was the Unit Master for Diploma School (Unit 6, 2004–09) and Intermediate School (Unit 2, 2002–04). He is pursuing his doctoral research at the Berlage Institute Rotterdam on the topic of the dominant type and the city. Serie, founded in 2007, is based in London, Mumbai, Beijing and Chengdu. The practice's theoretical interest lies in the relationship between dominant types and the city. The practice works typologically – thinking and designing in series – and is committed to the projection of the cumulative intelligence of types into architectural projects. The works of Serie have been exhibited and published widely. Serie is the UK BD Young Architect of the Year 2010–11.

**THURSDAY 19.05.2011
STÄDELSCHULE AULA
CÉCILE BRISAC**
BRISAC GONZALEZ (LONDON)
REAL JOY

Prior to co-founding Brisac Gonzalez, Cécile Brisac gained her experience in the design and implementation of large and complex projects working in the offices of Ian Ritchie Architects and RFR in London, as well as in France, Sweden and the United States. She is a graduate of the Architectural Association School of Architecture in London and a regular lecturer and guest juror in the UK, Scandinavia, the United States and France. She has won numerous awards such as the Chicago Athenaeum prize for European Architects in the US (the 40 under 40' award in Great Britain, and the Nouveaux Albums des Jeunes Architectes award in France. She has taught at the Architectural Association, and is a board member of the Southwark Design Review Panel in London.

**THURSDAY 26.05.2011
STÄDELSCHULE AULA
STEPHAN HENRICH**
AKADEMIE SCHLOSS SOLITUDE
(STUTTGART)
**MACHINIST PROTOCOLS
AND PROCESSES**

Stephan Henrich, currently a fellow at Akademie Schloss Solitude, Stuttgart, studied architecture and urban design at Universität Stuttgart. Since 2004, he has been working with RSI(e)n) Architects, Paris, where he is an associate for several projects including: "I've heard about", the Architectural Biennale, Venice (2008 and 2010, and "Une Architecture Des Humeurs". He has also worked for Kneppers/Helbig advanced engineering, Stuttgart and Schlaich Bergermann and Partners, Stuttgart. Henrich teaches at USC, Los Angeles, since 2009, where he is a subfounder of the LAB Mit with Francois Roche and Akis Mun. His research focuses on robotic design and the use of robotics in architecture. Previously, he has taught at the AA (Summer school 2006), at Die Angewandte, Vienna.

**WEDNESDAY 08.06.2011
STÄDELSCHULE AULA
METTE RAMSGARD THOMSEN**
*CENTRE FOR INFORMATION
TECHNOLOGY AND ARCHITEC-
TURE* (COPENHAGEN)
**DIGITAL PRACTICE: ADDRESSING
MATERIAL CULTURE**

Mette Ramsgard Thomsen's interest in architectural research revolves around digital technologies. Through a focus on intelligent programming and ideas of emergence she explores how computational logics can lead to new spatial concepts. Her work is practice lead and through projects she investigates the relationship between computational design, craft and technology. Her research focuses on digital crafting as way of thinking material practice, computation and fabrication as part of architectural culture. Ramsgard Thomsen is a Professor at the Royal Academy of Fine Arts, School of Architecture, in Copenhagen, where she heads the Centre for Information Technology and Architecture [CITA]. During the last 5 years she has successfully built the centre that now includes 14 active researchers and research students.

**THURSDAY 16.06.2011
STÄDELSCHULE AULA
SEAN AHLQUIST**
*INSTITUTE FOR COMPUTATIONAL
DESIGN, UNIVERSITY OF
STUTTGART*
**FORM: SYSTEMS OF SPATIAL
AND MATERIAL BEHAVIOR**

Sean Ahlquist is the founder of Proxi2, and currently a Research Associate and PhD Candidate of the Institute for Computational Design at the University of Stuttgart. Ahlquist has an MA from the AA. His work spans practice and theory. He has taught at UC Berkeley, California College of the Arts, and the AA. He has published widely on computational design and fabrication techniques, including a forthcoming book entitled *Computational Design Thinking*, co-edited with Achim Menges. Current research involves the development of computational methods which impose material characteristics through the calculation of fundamental physical behaviors. This involves the cross-disciplinary study of biology, biomimetic and structural engineering, material science and computation. His work embodies a strategy where computational design is the construction of various simulation technologies aimed at discovering innovative structural, material, climatic, and spatial principles, executed to resolve the complex integrated capacities that define architecture as a system of systems.

**06–08 JULY 2011
END-OF-YEAR PROGRAMME**

**06–08 JULY 2011
SAC MASTER THESIS AND
PROJECTS REVIEW 2011
DEUTSCHES ARCHITEKTUR-
MUSEUM FRANKFURT**

**FIRST YEAR GROUP
RESEARCH AND EXPERIMENTS:
INFORMED MATERIALITY**
14:00–18:30, JULY 6 AND
10:00–12:00, JULY 7

**MASTER THESIS GROUP
SESC CENTRE AT LUZ, SAO PAULO**
14:00–17:30, JULY 7 AND
10:00–17:00, JULY 8

**07–10 JULY 2011
SAC MASTER THESIS AND
PROJECTS EXHIBITION 2011
DEUTSCHES ARCHITEKTUR-
MUSEUM FRANKFURT
OPENING 18:00, JULY 7**

GÜNTER BOCK PRIZE
18:30, JULY 7 – SUPPORTED BY
THE STIFTUNG STÄDELSCHULE
FÜR BAUKUNST

**DEAN'S HONORARY LECTURE
PROFESSOR SANFORD KWINTER**
19:00, JULY 7
DEUTSCHES ARCHITEKTUR-
MUSEUM FRANKFURT
(GERMAN ARCHITECTURE
MUSEUM), SCHAUMAINKAI 43,
FRANKFURT

DAM DEUTSCHES ARCHITEKTURMUSEUM

Design of the 2011 conference and activities program for the Städelschule Architecture Class.

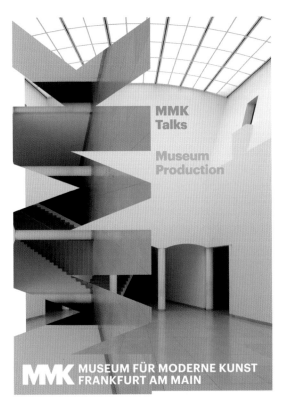

John Russo, Katrin Tüffers and Markus Weisbeck carried out the corporate design for the Museum of Modern Art in Frankfurt in 2010. With this change in the institution's brand image they managed for the design to be on par with the level of the contents.

Editorial design of a paperback collection for the New York and Berlin
Sternberg Press publishing house, in operation since 2000. Variations
have been designed for each of the 16 titles in the series.

Poster designed by Markus Weisbeck to mark the anniversary celebration of electronic music record label Rasyer Noton. A single series of 20 posters was printed.

Logo for the new Jewish Museum and the Museum of
the Jewish quarter of Frankfurt, where you can visit the
ruins of the old neighborhood. These logos renounce
the typical signs and symbols of Judaism and are based
on the location of the museums.

This iPhone application integrates the two most common views of clocks. It was for the first shown at the exhibition *The Beginning of the End of Time* at the Krome Gallery in Berlin.

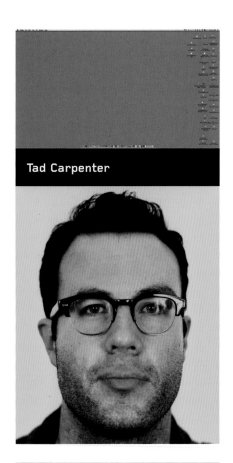

Tad Carpenter

Kansas City, MO, USA
www.tadcarpenter.com

Illustration for a poster advertising an exhibition of a cycling group.

I am an illustrator and designer living in sunny, snowy and forever changing Kansas City, Missouri in the United States of America. I have been lucky enough to work with clients such as: Macy's, Adobe, Chronicle Books, Target, Atlantic Records, Sunrise Greetings, The Corcoran Gallery of art in Washington D.C., Simon & Schuster, MTV, Conan O'Brien, Rayban, Anorak, Hallmark Cards, Kidrobot, Family Circle, Rayban, Myspace and Dave & Busters. I have illustrated and designed several children's books, spot illustrations and national campaigns in the current market place. I have been featured in *Communication Arts, Print, How, Graphis, Grain Edit, Drawn!, Design Sponge, Illustration Mundo* and dozens of publications in regards to design and illustration.

1. Examples of applications of illustrations and designs: small toys, cards, postcards etc.

2. Illustration for the home page of the designer's website.

ISSN 1727-417-6

8 (300) 2010

ГЕРОИ И ЖЕРТВЫ
ЦИФРОВОЙ РЕВОЛЮЦИИ

sf.kommersant.ru

Секрет фирмы

8 АВГУСТ

ИНВЕСТОПОЛИЯ
ПОСТРОЙ СВОЙ
БИЗНЕС
НА ЭЛЕКТРОННЫХ
КНИГАХ

ПИРАТСТВО

**НЕЗАЩИЩЕННОСТЬ
ПРОДАВАЕМЫХ КНИГ
ОТ КОПИРОВАНИЯ**

**ЧИТАТЕЛЬСКИЙ
ПОТЕНЦИАЛ**

ОБЪЕМ КНИГ, ПРОДАННЫХ
В 2009 ГОДУ, $ НА ЧЕЛОВЕКА

РОССИЯ: **0,2**
США: **0,9**

**НЕЗНАЧИТЕЛЬНЫЙ ОБЪЕМ ПОРТФЕЛЯ
ОЦИФРОВАННЫХ КНИГ**

КОЛИЧЕСТВО ОЦИФРОВАННЫХ КНИГ
У КРУПНЕЙШИХ ИГРОКОВ

РОССИЯ: **25 000***
США: **400 000****

* «Литрес»
** Amazon.com

**ПОТЕНЦИАЛ РОСТА
СТОИМОСТИ КНИГИ**

СРЕДНЯЯ ЦЕНА ЭЛЕКТРОННОЙ КНИГИ, $

РОССИЯ: **1**
США: **10**

ПОТЕНЦИАЛ РЫНКА

РЫНОК ЭЛЕКТРОННЫХ КНИГ
В 2009 ГОДУ, $ МЛН

РОССИЯ: **3***
США: **165**

* оценка «Литреса»

**НЕДОСТАТОЧНЫЙ УРОВЕНЬ
ПРОНИКНОВЕНИЯ ГАДЖЕТОВ**

УРОВЕНЬ ПРОНИКНОВЕНИЯ ГАДЖЕТОВ-
РИДЕРОВ, % ОТ НАСЕЛЕНИЯ

РОССИЯ: **0,2**
США: **0,9**

**ОТСУТСТВИЕ ЕДИНОГО
ФОРМАТА**

**КАК РОССИЙСКИЕ
КОМПАНИИ
ПРЕОДОЛЕВАЮТ
ЭТИ И ДРУГИЕ
ПРЕПЯТСТВИЯ** С. 62

Illustration for the cover of the business magazine published in Moscow *Sekret Firmy*.

Do Well by Doing Good is an illustration created for the music television channel MTV.

YEAH! BURGER

BURGERS & MORE

All of our patties are made with organic or natural ingredients and are free of antibiotics, hormones and preservatives.
All of our meats are humanely-raised. Our burgers and sandwiches are always cooked fresh, right when you order!

① CHOOSE YOUR PATTY

BEEF BURGER
A double stack of grass-fed, Georgia-raised beef
$6.99

BISON BURGER
Colorado grass-fed bison
$7.99

TURKEY BURGER
Certified organic turkey
$5.99

VEGGIE BURGER
Made with certified organic Sea Island red peas
$5.99

GRILLED CHICKEN BREAST SANDWICH
Certified organic chicken
$5.99

② CHOOSE YOUR BUN

SOUTHERN WHITE
Made with organic flour by H&F bakery

WHOLE WHEAT
Made with organic flour by H&F bakery

GLUTEN-FREE WHITE
Add $1.25

LETTUCE WRAP
Green leaf lettuce

③ TOP IT OFF!

ADD CHEESE!
Certified organic cheeses
$1 EACH

AMERICAN
BLUE
CHEDDAR

PEPPER JACK
PIMENTO
SWISS

FREE TOPPINGS
Go for it!

LETTUCE
TOMATO
DILL PICKLES
JALAPEÑOS

CHOPPED VIDALIA ONIONS *Organic*
SLICED VIDALIA ONIONS *Organic*
GRILLED VIDALIA ONIONS *Organic*
SUNFLOWER SPROUTS

PREMIUM TOPPINGS
$1 EACH

NITRATE-FREE BACON
TURKEY BACON
SAUTÉED MUSHROOMS
CAGE-FREE FRIED EGG *Organic*

SLICED AVOCADO
SHAUN'S RED CHILI
NAPA COLESLAW

④ GET SAUCED!

All sauces are FREE on your burger or sandwich! Try as a dipping sauce with fries for $.50 EACH.

YEAH! SAUCE
KETCHUP
MUSTARD

HONEY MUSTARD
DUKE'S MAYO
HOT ALABAMA RELISH

ROASTED GARLIC BBQ
BACON JAM
BLACK PEPPERCORN STEAK

MISSISSIPPI MOP BBQ
WHITE BBQ
ROOSTER SAUCE

HOT DOGS

Featuring Let's Frank all-natural hot dogs!
Served on a Southern White bun made with organic flour

THE CLASSIC $4.99
Grass-fed beef hot dog with your choice of toppings from above

SOUTHERN DOG $5.99
Grass-fed beef hot dog topped with Pimento cheese, chopped Vidalia onions and hot Alabama relish

CHILI & CHEESE DOG $5.99
Grass-fed beef hot dog topped with Shaun's red chili, organic American cheese and jalapenos

SIDES $2.49 EACH
Add dipping sauce for $.50!
We use 100% heart-healthy canola oil for our fries, onion rings and pickles!

HAND-CUT FRENCH FRIES
GLUTEN-FREE FRENCH FRIES
BUTTERMILK VIDALIA ONION RINGS
FIFTY-FIFTY
Half French fries, half onion rings

FRIED PICKLES
KETTLE POTATO CHIPS $1.49
CUP OF SHAUN'S RED CHILI
CUP OF NAPA COLESLAW

SALADS
All of our salads are made with organic lettuce!

SIMPLE GREENS $5.99
Lettuce, cucumber, radish and fresh herb lemon vinaigrette
WITH GRILLED ORGANIC CHICKEN $9.99

CAESAR SALAD $5.99
Lettuce, croutons, Parmigiano cheese and Caesar dressing
WITH GRILLED ORGANIC CHICKEN $9.99

CLASSIC COBB $9.99
Lettuce, avocado, nitrate-free bacon, grilled organic chicken, hardboiled egg, organic blue cheese crumbles and Johnston Family Farms buttermilk ranch dressing

KIDDIE COMBOS
All Kiddie Combos come with french fries, choice of an organic milk box or organic apple juice

BURGER COMBO $6.99
Single patty grass-fed beef burger

HOT DOG COMBO $6.99
Grass-fed beef hot dog

 ICE CREAM
Featuring Strauss Family Creamery organic soft-serve ice cream!

MILK SHAKES
Made with certified organic milk!
$4.99 EACH

CHOCOLATE
VANILLA
STRAWBERRY
PEACH
COFFEE
COOKIES AND CREAM
WHYNATTE

FLOATS
Featuring Boylan sodas with 100% cane sugar
$4.99 EACH

BROWN COW
Vanilla ice cream with Root Beer
BLACK COW
Vanilla ice cream with Black Cherry soda
CREAMSICLE
Vanilla ice cream with Orange soda

CONCRETES $4.99 EACH
Vanilla soft-serve ice cream blended at high speed with your favorite mix-ins!
Your first mix-in is free! Add more for $.50 EACH.

MIX-INS
HOT FUDGE
COOKIES AND CREAM
PEANUT BUTTER CUPS

CHOPPED PEANUTS
PEANUT BRITTLE
HEATH CANDY BAR

CHOCOLATE ALMOND BARK
CHOCOLATE ESPRESSO BEANS

SUNDAES $4.99 EACH
Your choice of CHOCOLATE or VANILLA soft-serve ice cream in a cup with HOT FUDGE, CHOPPED PEANUTS and FRESH WHIPPED CREAM

CUPS $2.99 EACH
Your choice of CHOCOLATE or VANILLA soft-serve ice cream

 BEVERAGES
Alcoholic

BEER

DRAFTS

	GLASS	PITCHER
BROWN LAGER Brooklyn Brewery	$5	$18
DOPPELBOCK Spaten Optimator	$5	$18
INDIA PALE ALE Harpoon	$5	$18
PALE ALE Sweetwater 420	$5	$18
TRIPEL ALE Chimay White	$8	$30

BOTTLES & CANS

INDIA PALE ALE Bison IPA *Organic*		$5
LAGER Pabst Blue Ribbon		$3
LAGER Budweiser		$3
LIGHT LAGER Bud Light		$3
LIGHT LAGER Amstel Light		$4
PALE LAGER Stella Artois		$5
GLUTEN-FREE Green's Amber Ale		$8

WINE

RED WINES

CABERNET SAUVIGNON Leese-Fitch, Sonoma '08	$8
MALBEC Yellow+Blue, Argentina '08 *Organic*	$8
PINOT NOIR Wild Hog, Russian River Valley '06	$8
SYRAH Qupé, Central California Coast '07	$12

WHITE WINES

CHARDONNAY Estancia, Monterey County '08	$8
PINOT GRIGIO Casa Delia, Italy '08	$8
ROSÉ Domaine de Nizas, France '08	$8
SAUVIGNON BLANC Yellow+Blue, Chile '08 *Organic*	$8

SIGNATURE COCKTAILS

MARGARITA Conquistador tequila, triple sec, lime and Hawaiian sea salt	$8
MOJITO Cruzan rum, muddled mint and lime	$8
FROZEN STRAWBERRY DAIQUIRI Rum, strawberries, lemon and ice	$8
RUBY RED EYE Absolut Ruby Red vodka, Campari and fresh grapefruit juice	$9
CRITICAL MASS Tuaca liqueur, Chimay White beer and fresh orange juice	$9
COMSTOCK MULE High West Silver whiskey, ginger beer and lime	$9
DARK & STORMY Gosling's Black Rum, ginger beer and lime	$8
FATHER'S OFFICE Johnnie Walker Red whiskey, Cherry Heering, fresh orange juice	$9
RYE TOAST Old Overholt Rye whiskey, Cynar liqueur and lemon bitters	$8
MANHATTAN Russell's Reserve Rye, sweet vermouth and bitters	$8

SPIRITS

GIN

GORDON'S	$6
BEEFEATER	$8

RUM

CAPTAIN MORGAN	$7
CRUZAN	$7
HORNÉ SPICED RUM	$8
GOSLING'S BLACK RUM	$8

TEQUILA

CONQUISTADOR	$7
PATRON SILVER	$10

VODKA

PRAIRIE ORGANIC	$7
GREY GOOSE	$9
BELVEDERE	$10

WHISKIES

OLD OVERHOLT	$6
EVAN WILLIAMS	$6
FOUR ROSES SM. BATCH	$7
JACK DANIEL'S	$8
JAMESON	$8
JOHNNIE WALKER RED	$8
RUSSELL'S RESERVE RYE	$8
BASIL HAYDEN'S	$9
MAKER'S MARK	$9
HIGH WEST SILVER	$9
HIGH WEST RENDEZVOUS	$10
WOODFORD RESERVE	$10

BEVERAGES
Non-Alcoholic

SODA

DRAFTS $1.75
Featuring Coca-Cola products
COKE
DIET COKE
COKE ZERO
SPRITE
MELLOW YELLOW
DR. PEPPER
BARQ'S ROOT BEER

BOTTLES $2
Boylan sodas made with 100% cane sugar
ROOT BEER
ORANGE
CREAM
BLACK CHERRY

TEA

BREWED $1.75
Revolution Tea iced teas
SWEET TEA
UNSWEETENED TEA

BOTTLED $2
GREEN TEA *Organic*

OTHER DRINKS

JUICES

ORANGE JUICE Fresh-squeezed	$3
GRAPEFRUIT JUICE Fresh-squeezed	$3
ORGANIC APPLE JUICE POUCH	$2

SPARKLING BEVERAGES

IZZE Clementine	
IZZE Peach	

ENERGY DRINKS

RED BULL	$2.50
RED BULL SUGAR-FREE	$2.50
WHYNATTE	$3.25

VITAMIN WATER $2
LEMONADE Multi-V
ORANGE Essential
TROPICAL CITRUS Energy

WATER

FILTERED WATER	FREE
BOTTLED WATER FIJI	$1.75
SPARKLING WATER San Pellegrino	$2

MILK $2
Horizon organic milk boxes
CHOCOLATE
STRAWBERRY
WHITE

1388 Howell Mill Road | Suite E
Atlanta, Georgia | 30318
P 404.496.4282 | F 404.496.4968
facebook.com/yeahburger | twitter.com/yeahburger
YEAHBURGER.COM

 FRESH

WELCOME TO YEAH! BURGER

Design of the image for a burger franchise Yeah Burger: menus, wall murals and illustrations for T-shirts and badges, among other products.

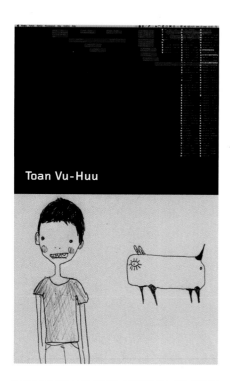

Toan Vu-Huu

Paris, France
www.toanvuhuu.com

I was born in Germany, where I graduated in visual communications. I worked for five years at the design studio Intégral Ruedi Baur and associates in Paris, specializing in the creation of visual identities and signage systems such as the ones at the Centre Pompidou in Paris. At Intégral, I was in charge of projects such as the Cologne Bonn Airport and La Cinémathèque Française. In 2005, I opened my own design studio. Our clients come mainly from the cultural field, like museums, libraries, schools, art magazines, book editors, artists and galleries. We work in the fields of corporate identity, signage systems, editorial design, scenography and museography. In 2006, I also became lecturer in typography at the École nationale supérieure des arts décoratifs in Paris. Since 2008 I have been working, together with my associate André Baldinger, in different projects for Baldinger Vu-Huu.

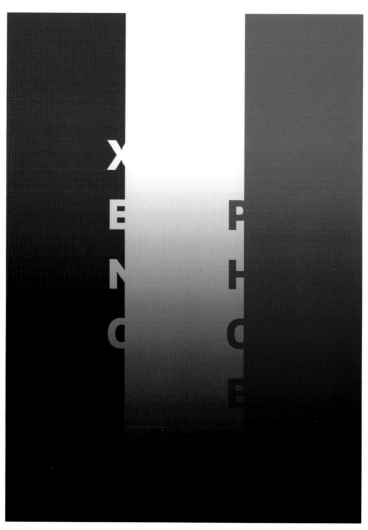

Design of a promotional poster for an exhibition denouncing the alleged xenophobia of French politicians.

First volume of the complete catalog of the work by the French artist Christian Boltanski, written and compiled by Bob Calle.

POOR

SERVICES

Vernissage le vendredi 11.02.11 à 18h

Exposition du 12 au 20.02.11 de 15h à 18h

Julie Brenot
Georgina Criddle
Mathurin Théodose
François Fleury
Nadine Fraczkowski
Jérôme Guigue
Sloan Leblanc
Stéphanie Lefebvre
Pierre Limpens
Frédérique Manceau
Nicolas Milhé
Arnika Müll
Hank Schmidt in der Beek
Rouven Schmitt
X'O_54 feat. Dominique Forest
(une performance en partenariat
avec Poor Services)

La Générale en Manufacture
6 Grande Rue
92310 Sèvres

3

Métro 9
Pont de Sèvres
Tram 2
Musée de Sèvres

POOR

SERVICES

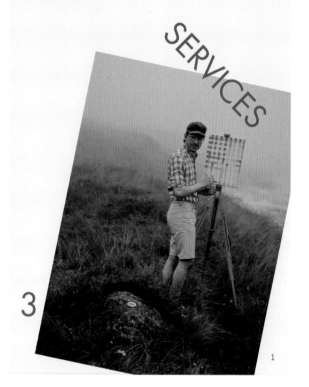

3

1

2

1. Flyer for the group exhibition *Poor Service 3* at the La Générale Manufacture residence.

2. Design of flyer and business card for the Élizabeth Naudet and Luc Poux Architects studio.

Catalogue for the Lebanese artist Walid Raad. It compiles several bomb blasts, a common occurrence in Lebanon in 2006.

Christmas greetings in the form of calendar for Ante
Prima Conseil. On each of the double pages two weeks
in separate rows are represented. The yellow band
indicates the number of hours of sun each day.

Catalog design for the project *Amnesia-Memoria* by the secondary art school in Amiens (ESAD) and Bauhaus University in Weimar.

Tomaž Plahuta

Nova Gorica, Slovenia
www.tomazplahuta.com

I am an art director and freelance visual communications designer juggling many roles, from designing books and managing one of the most renowned Slovenian publishing houses, to coordinating and developing some of the Slovenian and Macedonian wine brands... But life is much more than just design and its beautiful and colorful world. I am an extremist searching for utmost endurance and flexibility of the mind and body. I am switching from leisure to total strain. I am a dreamer and traveler within many dimensions that normal eyes could not even begin to imagine. In the end it is love that counts. And peace.

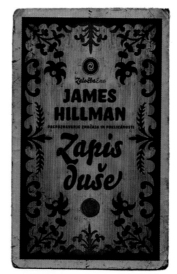

Editorial design book by James Hillman *Zapis duše*. The book talks about the path that a soul must travel between the time of birth and death.

5

In the book *Misli ob kuhinjski mizi* by Rachel Naomi Remen, kitchen tile images are used.

Editorial design is one of Tomaž Plahuta's specialties. Floral motifs and symbolic elements from the texts are used on the covers of books by Sergio Bambaren and the psychoanalyst Clarissa Pinkola Estés.

The symbol of a bouquet of flowers was chosen to symbolize the compilation of stories from the book *Umetnost življenja* by Epiktet.

ZALOŽBA ENO

TEŽA METULJA
ERRI
DE LUCA

Book written by the Italian ascetic Erri de Luca. Interpreting its minimalist language and translating it through graphic design was a challenge for the designer.

ZALOŽBA ENO

TRIJE KONJI
ERRI
DE LUCA

ZALOŽBA ENO

**CASTIGO PARA LOS
QUE NO PRACTICAN
SU PUREZA CON
FEROCIDAD.***

MARIO TREJO
Argentina 1926

*GORJE JIM, KI NISO SUROVO ČISTI V SVOJIH DEJANJIH.

-3-

TRIJE KONJI

BEREM samo rabljene knjige.

Prislonim jih na košarico za kruh, s prstom obrnem stran, da obleži. Tako žvečim in berem.

Nove knjige so nadležne, listi se samovoljno obračajo, upirajo se in treba jih je pritisniti, da obstanejo. Rabljene knjige imajo zrahljana rebra, strani prebiraš, ne da bi se nenehno dvigale.

Opoldne sedem na isti stol v gostilni, naročim minéštro in vino in berem.

Berem romane o morju, dogodivščinah v gorah, nobenih zgodb o mestih, ki jih imam okoli sebe.

Malce dvignem oči zaradi sončnega odseva na steklu vhodnih vrat, skozi katera vstopita, ona vsa

-7-

Trije konji, by Erri de Luca.

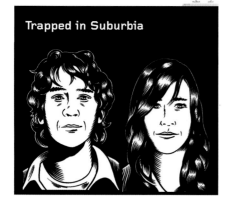

WORK HARDER YOU BASTERD!

Trapped in Suburbia

The Hague, the Netherlands
www.trappedinsuburbia.com

Trapped in Suburbia was born in 2004 in Mariahoeve, a suburb of The Hague. It all started with us (Cuby Gerards and Karin Langeveld) working from our home, a tiny apartment. And because we like our humor to shine through in our work we thought it was a good idea to add a little humor to the name as well. Hence the name Trapped in Suburbia. We are now located in the old Caballero Factory, hub of creativity and a very inspiring place to be. Cuby studied Photography, Graphic & Typographic Design at the Royal Academy of Arts in The Hague. He studied Applied Creativity at the Hallo academy. Karin studied Graphic & Typographic Design at the Royal Academy of Arts in The Hague and got her masters degree in Design at the Sandberg Institute in Amsterdam. We love telling stories and inspiring people, conducting extensive research and pushing boundaries. We drink from a cup that's half empty and have fun.

AnalogFest is a festival that celebrates analogue techniques with workshops, exhibitions, party and lectures by artists like Anthony Burrill and Jon Burgerman.

Posters by Anthony Burrill, Joe Buergerman, Zeloot and
Trapped in Suburbia.

DESIGN IT YOURSELF

B☐ GRAPHIC DESIGN MUSEUM

ON THE COVER

STOP WE HAVE MOTION

BACK TO THE DRAWING BOARD

DESIGN -O-MAT

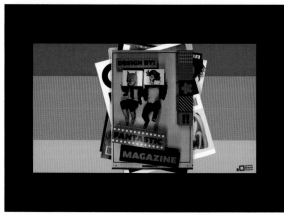

Design it Yourself is an exhibition which invites visitors to design magazines, t-shirts or animations frame by frame.

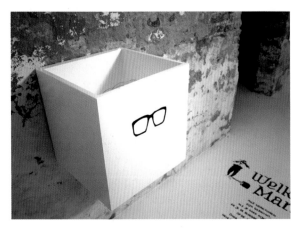

This exhibition redesigns a torture chamber using UV
paint, which is displayed by focusing on it a UV flashlight.
You use the light to view the exhibition, discovering what
lurks behind each corner.

The *Trapped in Suburbia* exhibition won first prize in the
European Design Awards in 2012 and came second in
the International Design Awards, in 2009 .

Work a Lot is a flexible office that can be rented for short periods of time. The decorative posters include phrases that motivate the worker.

The company Suited Concepts creates new concepts for old buildings. The campaign plays with the idea of giving voice to the buildings, as if they could express their preferences.

Where there is smoke, there is fire is a publication on the old Caballero Tobacco Factory, transformed into a business incubator. This book won the second prize of the European Design Awards 2009 in the category of book covers.

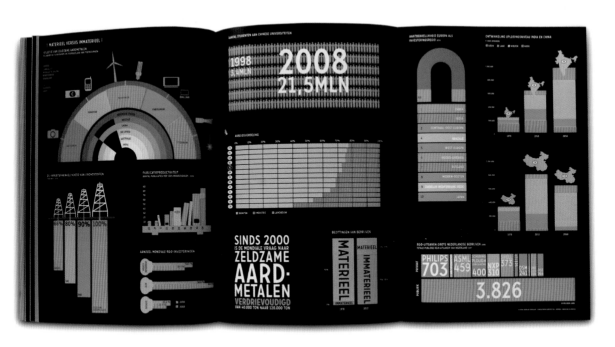

This publication, designed for the Knowledge Economy Monitor displays the current economic situation in the Netherlands through computer graphics and bright colors .

Triboro

New York, NY, USA
www.triborodesign.com

Triboro is the husband and wife team of David Heasty and Stefanie Weigler. Triboro creates design solutions for clients in publishing, art, fashion, music, lifestyle, and for cultural institutions. The studio excels both in building inspiring brands from the ground-up and in shepherding established brands into new territories. Triboro's partners have won numerous industry awards and their work has been featured in publications and exhibitions around the world.

Art Direction for a special issue of the magazine *GQ* entitled *GQ Style Manual*.

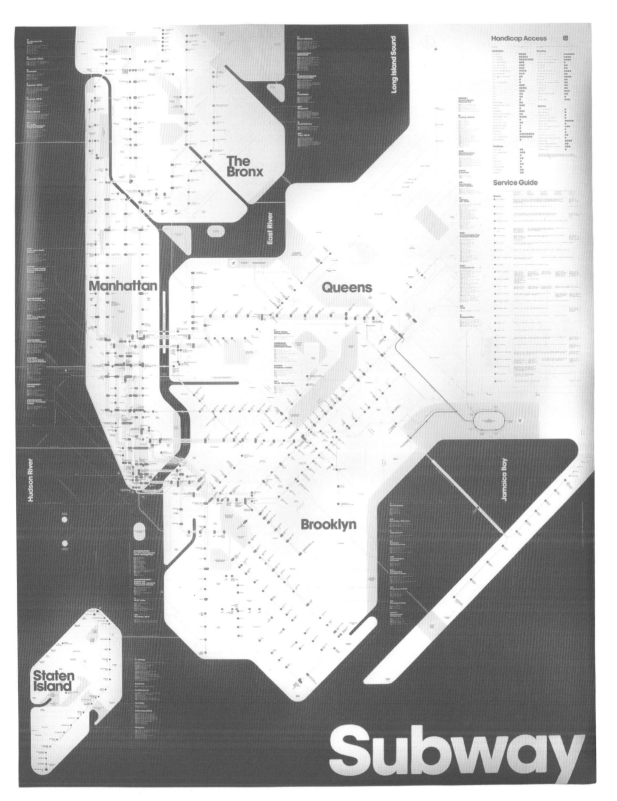

Limited edition large format poster for the New York Metro, printed in red neon.

Cover design for *New York Magazine*. This is a special issue with the
theme *Best of NY*.

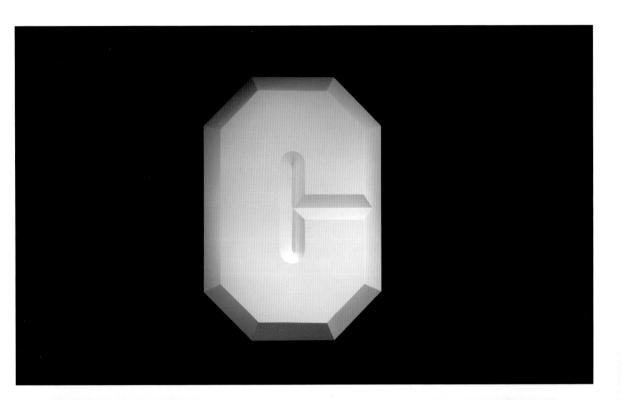

Invitation to the group exhibition *Built To Survive the Real World* held in Roth Gallery in New York.

Design of the brand image of the William Rast fashion label created by Justin Timberlake and Trace Ayala.

Collection of unpublished projects: typography, posters, sketches etc.

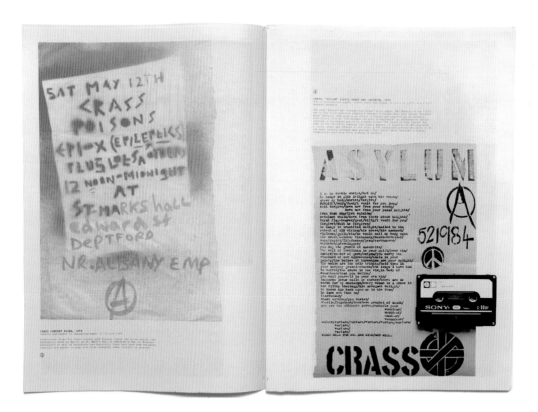

Design of exhibition catalog on the band
Crass in the Roth Gallery.

Poster for an auction and exhibition at the Type Director's Club of New York.

Version Industries

London, UK,
New York, NY, USA
www.versionindustries.com

I am a graphic designer, photographer and film maker. I was born in London in 1979. I co-founded Version Industries in 2003 when I was 23. I have remained Creative Director and lead designer for the company since it's inception producing websites, printwork and video pieces for clients like Daft Punk, Jennifer Lopez, Disney, Saatchi + Saatchi, Topspin and David Yurman. Over the years we've shown a particularly astute understanding of musicians and filmmakers and I myself spend most of my free time art directing bands and giving independent filmmakers the support they need online. My critical writings on design and advertising have earned the respect of such design luminaries as David Carson. My parents are both fine artists and I have no formal training in design.

65DAYSOFSTATIC
WE WERE EXPLODING ANYWAY

ESCAPE FROM NEW YORK

DAYSOFSTATIC

Design of several posters for the presentation of documentaries, tours and the group's fourth album 65daysofstatic, British math rock and post-rock band.

Illustration for the album *Blue*, the first by the group Sonoio, the solo musical project by Alessandro Cortini, formerly of the band Nine Inch Nails.

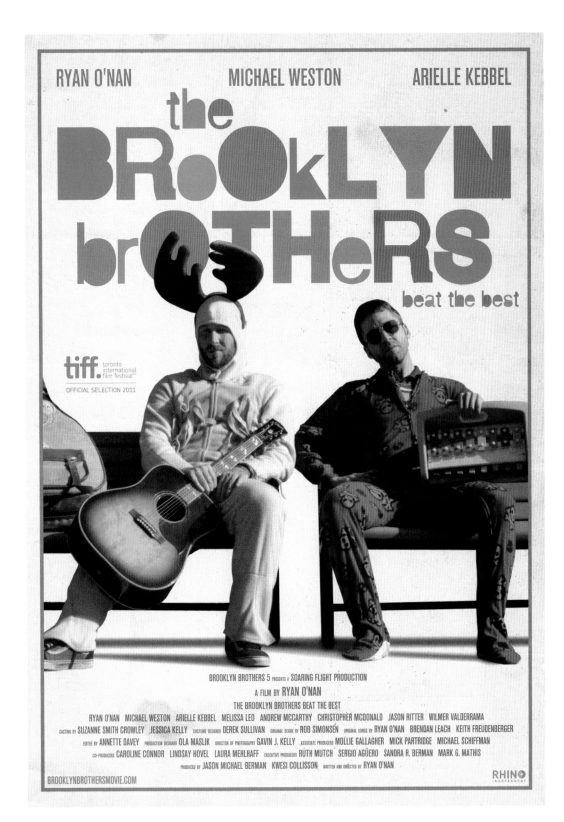

Poster for the romantic comedy *The Brooklyn Brothers Beat the Best*, directed by and starring Ryan O'Nan.

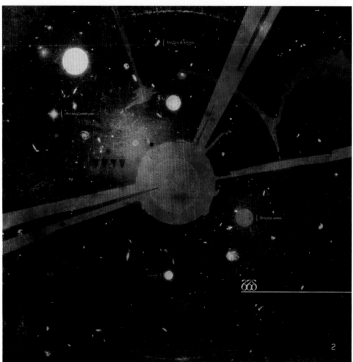

1. Cover design of the first LP by Polinski, *Labyrinths*, published in vinyl.

2. Cover design of the first LP by Big Black Delta, *BBDLP1*.

The design of CD covers and posters for bands is one of the specialties of this design studio. This time, it's a cover and a poster for the band Mellowdrone, for the presentation of its second LP, *Angry Bear*.

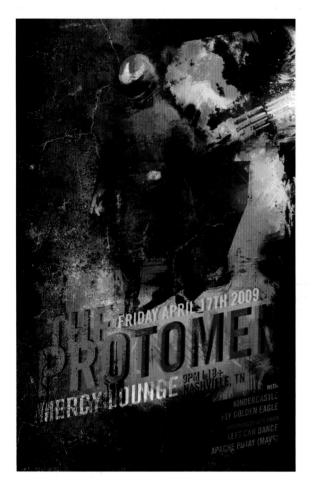

Design of posters to promote the second studio album by
the group The Protoman, *Act II. The Father of Death*, and
the concert they performed in Nashville.

Poster design for the group's tour of the west coast of the USA.

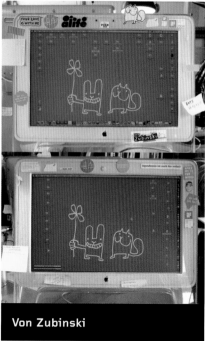

Von Zubinski

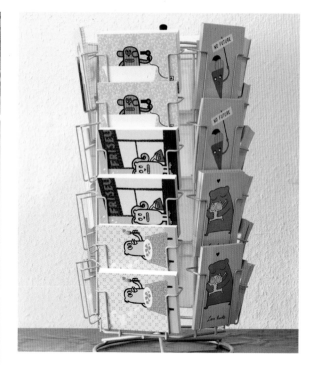

Frankfurt, Germany
www.vonZubinski.com

Some of the ideas of the components of the studio ultimately become screenprints and others postcards or stickers. They are sold in the store Colekt in Frankfurt.

We are two graphic designers from Frankfurt, Germany. In 2001, we founded our studio, Von Zubinski. Over the years our focus shifted more and more from classic graphic design to illustration. Now we are mostly known for our cute and weird little characters and our typographic prints. To show-case our illustrations to a greater audience we established the sub label Zubinski Products in 2010. Under this name we produce and sell jewelry, fashion and artworks. Together with our friends from the studio Labor we created several doodle books for children, more than 100.000 copies were sold in Germany.

STOP RAINING ON ME

ADD ME AS A FRIEND

I LIKE SOCK EXCH ANGE

WAKE ME FOR MEALS

1. The painted cardboard boxes are transformed into objects and characters.

2. Illustration about dental health, teeth are painted cardboard boxes.

With more cardboard boxes, the designers built this eyecatching giant three meter hairy structure.

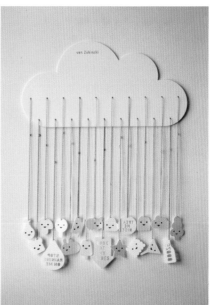

Design of acrylic jewelry made in collaboration with an industrial design studio. To date more than 20 different pieces have been designed, although the collection will be extended.

Design of children's books-notebooks to scribble in, in collaboration with the Labor studio.

Vruchtvlees

The Hague, the Netherlands
www.vruchtvlees.com

We are a passionate graphic design studio. We provide creative communication for different media. With great enthusiasm we develop websites, brochures, corporate identities, logo design, posters, annual reports, brochures and magazines. We started in 2007 in The Hague. During our studies at the Royal Academy of Arts, we (Roman Stikkelorum, Michael Danker and Rindor Golverdingen) orchestrated our graphic design studio. Each person has its own field of expertise. Rindor does the illustration work, Michael is responsible for the photography and Roman is responsible for typography. We work for clients such as Nederlands Dans Theater, Heineken, Paard van Troje, *Blend Magazine* and Bart B More.

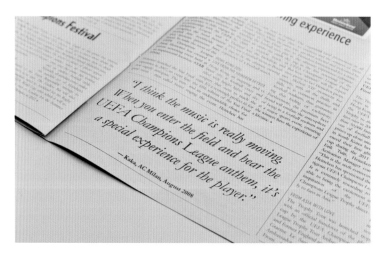

Newspaper specially designed by the Heineken brewery to mark the end of the Champions League held at Wembley Stadium in London.

Corporate image for the fashion festival It's Like
ZoOnwijs Freaking Fabuloos.

Design of the mockup issue of the literary magazine *Das Magazin*.

Current and vintage fashion market poster Le Grand Marche.

DE VLEESCH-HOUWERIJ

SOWIESO WERKEN WE NATUURLIJK OOK GRAAG MET DE INPUT VAN ONZE KLANTEN

www.wrangler.com

www.g.sherman.com

www.goodscraft.nl

www.riverisland.com

www.laperla.com

TATTOOS

ВОЛЯ К ВЛАСТИ

KIM PAPANATOS

Voordat Kim zich op het tatoeëren stortte was hij, nadat hij het Grafisch Lyceum af had gerond, vooral werkzaam als vormgever in de reclamewereld. "Dat heeft natuurlijk verder helemaal niks met tatoeëren te maken maar je leert wel andere mensen hun opdrachten te realiseren en een bepaalde manier van vormgeven. Het verschil is dat in de tattoowereld over het algemeen zowel de klant als de uitvoerder

allebei blij moeten zijn met het ontwerp dat uiteindelijk word gebruikt. In de reclamewereld moet je vooral doen wat je wordt opgedragen, ook al vind je het spuuglelijk. Als tatoeëerder zal je daar minder snel in toegeven, en is het over het algemeen toch werk waar je ook echt achter staat. Ook als de klant bijvoorbeeld een bepaalde tekst wilt in een bepaald type probeer je er toch net even je eigen draai aan te geven".

Papanatos presents : DE VLEESSCHOUWERIJ —weimarstraat 32

page 3

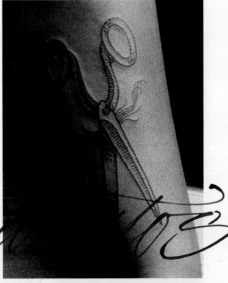

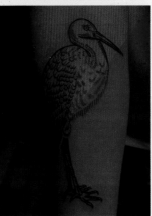

"IK WILDE OOK GRAAG EEN SHOP WAAR MENSEN MAKKELIJK NAAR BINNEN LOPEN VOOR DE KLEINE.." MET DE KINDEREN? WE GRAPPEN AL DAT JE DE KINDVRIENDELIJKSTE TATTOOSHOP VAN DEN HAAG BENT "JA, IK DOE DAAR NIET MOEILIJK OVER, KINDEREN ZIJN OOK NET MENSEN…"

Regular publication of the Papanatos tattoo studio. Photography by Koen Veldman.

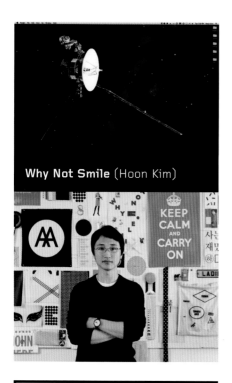

Why Not Smile (Hoon Kim)

New York, NY, USA
http://whynotsmile.com

Why Not Smile is a graphic design workshop in New York. We focus on design for art, architecture and cultural clients across various media: printed matter, branding, exhibition design, motion graphics, and websites. We have earned recognition from various organizations such as Art Directors Club, AIGA Best 50 Books, Brno Graphic Design Biennial and Chaumont Poster and Graphic Design. Prior to forming Why Not Smile, I have worked for the Museum of Modern Art (MoMA), Practise and Samsung Design Membership. I hold an MFA from Rhode Island School of Design, a teaching certificate from Brown University, and a BFA from Seoul National University, Korea. I have taught at Harvard University, Pratt Institute and RISD and given lectures Royal College of Art in London. I have been awarded as The Design Leader by the Ministry of Knowledge Economy of Korea and the Korea Institute of Design Promotion.

Identity design, web and brochures for the conferences on the sustainable future of the Exumas archipelago.

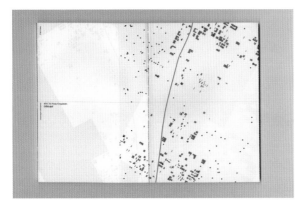

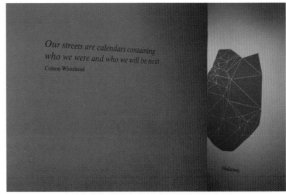

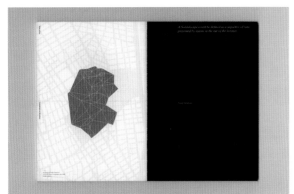

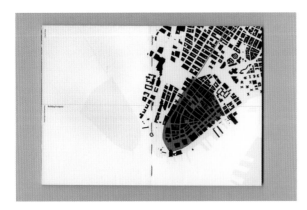

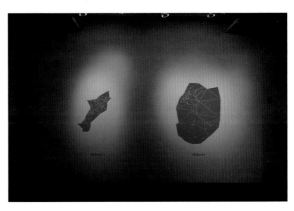

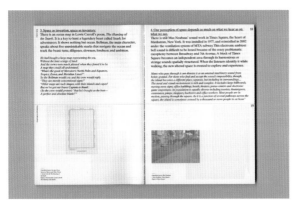

Book design and exposition *Walk on Red: Soundscapes on Broadway*, which shows the four neighborhoods adjacent to the Broadway Avenue and collects the complaints for excessive noise. With collaboration from Sarah Williams.

FEB 12
5:30 PM
PRATT MANHATTAN
ROOM 213

SULKI-MIN.COM

SPRING 2010
DESIGN LECTURE SERIES
GRAD COMD

Pratt

Poster for the Sulki & Min conference in the Pratt Institute in New York.

Mannam
**Five Graphic Dialogues
in New York**

만남
뉴욕의 다섯가지
그래픽 다이알로그

Mannam
In partnership with the design-oriented
fashion shops Project No. 8 and 8b,
Mannam (Korean for *meeting*) investigates
the relationships between Korean and non-
Korean designers. Participants are invited
to start with one-on-one dialogues, and to
generate form that responds to both their
developing dialogue, and the context of the
commercial space. Recording or keeping
a record of these dialogues in some way is
required, and at the project's completion,
the curators will search the transcripts for
significant moments, engage in a dialogue
of our own, and publish a survey and
archive of the project.
　　Mannam is an experimental method for
the generation and exhibition of original
work by graphic designers. We believe that
the displayable and interpretable work of
a graphic designer should not be limited
to a discrete and familiar "deliverable", but
can be broadened to include their research,
their self-education, their thought process,
etc. In the end, Mannam is an opportunity
to publicly present work of designers
we admire.

Exhibition
February 28—March 26 2010
Project No. 8: 138 Division St
Project No. 8b: 38 Ochard St

Hours
Tuesday—Sunday, 1—7 PM
Closed Monday

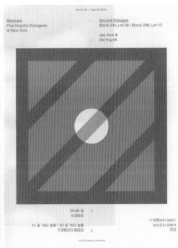

The designers carried out the
design and acted as curators at the
exhibition *Mannam: Five Dialogues
in New York*, which investigates
the relationship between Koreans
and non-Korean designers. In
collaboration with Andrew Sloat.

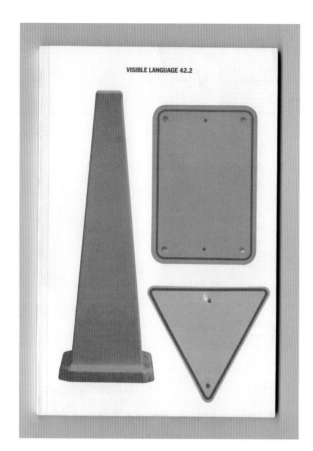

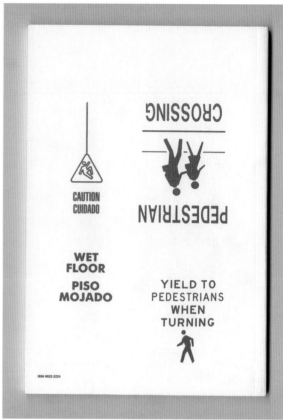

ISSN 0022-2224

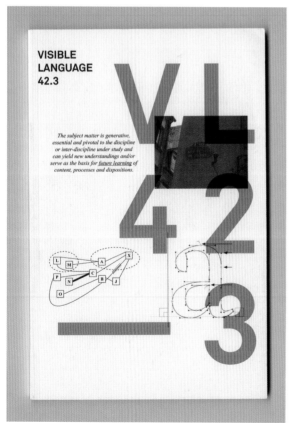

VISIBLE
LANGUAGE
42.3

The subject matter is generative, essential and pivotal to the discipline or inter-discipline under study and can yield new understandings and/or serve as the basis for future learning of content, processes and dispositions.

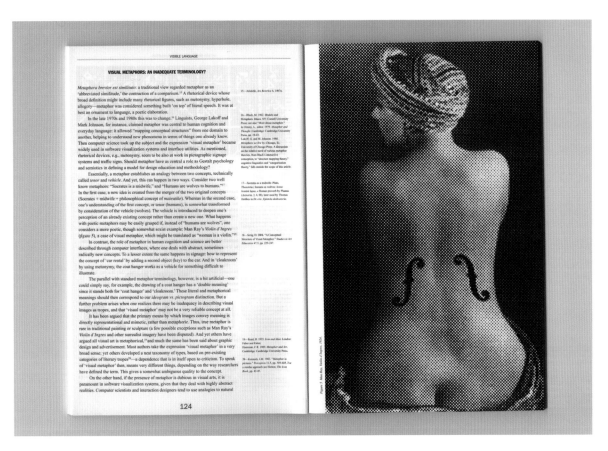

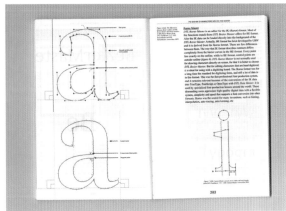

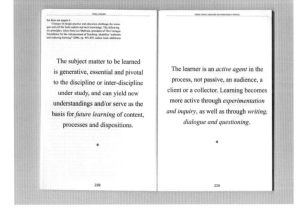

Visible Language is a publication that investigates and attempts to define the role and properties of written language. The designers designed the numbers 42.2 and 42.3.

WVDV (Willem van de Ven, Walewijn den Boer)

Amsterdam, the Netherlands
www.studiowvdv.nl

We are design websites and print solutions for various companies and organizations, mainly in the cultural and socially innovative field. Our work is generally content driven and dynamic. Influenced by the unstoppable progression of interactive possibilities in new-media, we aim to translate many of these interactive aspects into printwork for example by making alternative non-linear navigation structures within books. And we love our job.

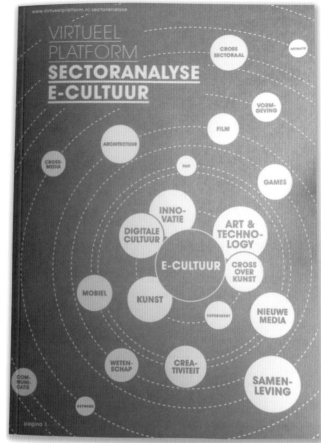

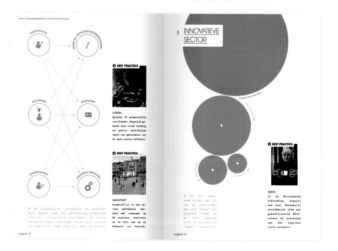

Sector Analysis is a publication by Virtueel Platform, the Institute for Digital Culture.

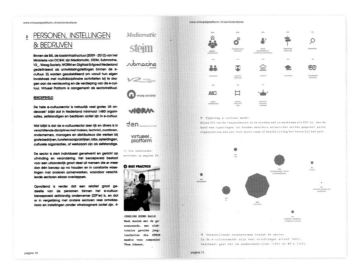

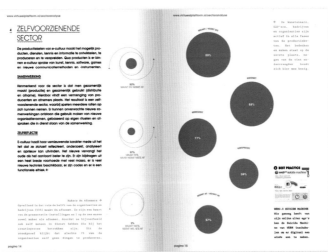

This publication focuses on all types of digital platforms for the dissemination of culture.

Pal Penthouse is a project in which teenagers build their ideal apartment in a four day period. Members of the WVDV studio designed the posters.

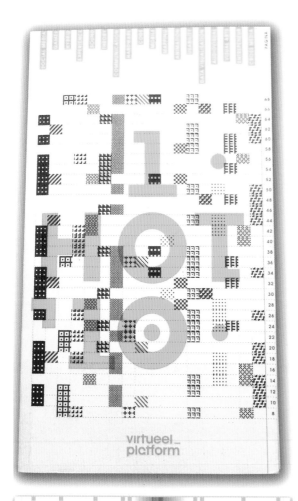

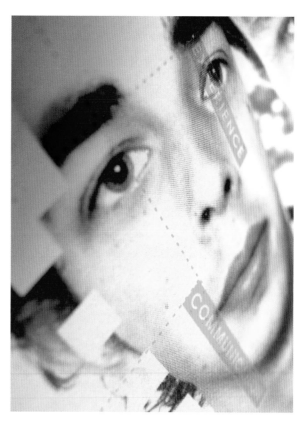

Book design *Hot 100*. This book is a compilation of the most outstanding students in Communication Studies in which the student profiles are organized based on their skills.

Alphabet designed from images of buildings in the neighborhood of New West in Amsterdam.

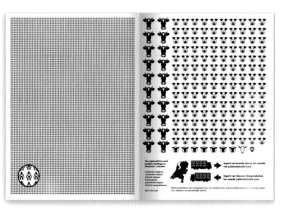

Kost is a book composed of essays, interviews, illustrations and various articles by designers, artists and scientists who deal with the value of food.

Design of a poster for a meeting of entrepreneurs in the neighborhood of Amsterdam West.